Wait
Wat

Seren Drama

Waiting at the Water's Edge

Lucinda Coxon

Edited by Brian Mitchell

seren

seren
is the book imprint of
Poetry wales Press Ltd.
First Floor, 2 Wyndham Street,
Bridgend, Mid Glamorgan,
Wales, CF31 1EF

© Lucinda Coxon, 1993
First published in 1995

For production rights contact
A.P. Watt Ltd., 20 John Street, London

Cataloguing In Publication Data for this book
is available from the British Library

ISBN 1-85411-149-3

The publisher acknowledges the finanical assistance of the
Arts Council of Wales' Drama Department

Cover by Andy Dark

Printed by The Cromwell Press
Melksham

Introduction

My grandmother, Edna May Bibby, was born in Rhydyfelan on March 18th, 1906 and moved to England, along with two of her sisters, to work in service around 1920. All three of them spent the remainder of their adult lives in England, settling quite early on in Derby. They returned to Wales only for family visits and holidays but dreamt always, and especially in their later years, of 'going home'.

Of course, the truth is that there was no longer a 'home' that they really recognised. Time had taken care of that. But all this meant that I grew up with a powerful sense of something lost — to them, to my father, and consequently to me. A sense of language and of landscape and of lives, from which we were all now effectively exiled. What had begun as straightforward economic migrancy became translated into a far more complex dynamic operating within us. And when I finally left Derby and moved to London — again, largely drawn by work opportunities — I began to feel what I believed to be something of my grandmother and great aunts' emotional journey repeating itself in me.

There is a moment in *Waiting at the Water's Edge* when Vi and Su are talking about moving to England and Vi says "once you've gone you can't come back". In some ways she is right. We can't go back in any simple sense. But time and the human heart do not operate simply, and one of the things that Vi discovers in the play is that she can, in fact, "change the past".

Waiting at the Water's Edge has, in personal terms, "changed the past" for me and perhaps for my family a little bit too. I would like also to think that it has in some way brought the spirit of my grandmother and her sisters home again and united us all in the kind of eternal present that the women of this play finally come to enjoy.

I would also like to thank the Soho Poly, Tricycle, Royal Court and Bush theatres for their support at various stages in the development of the piece and also Loose Exchange Theatre Company with whom the play began its life. In addition, I am indebted to Polly Teale, Kate Damelson, Sir Anthony Hopkins and NCE Wright without whom the Bush production would have been impossible.

Helen Anderson first played Su back in 1988 when there was only a five-minute fragment of a scene in existence. That this fragment turned out to be the starting point for a much bigger journey is largely due to the things I have learned from working with her.

Lucinda Coxon

For Paul

Notes to the Original Production

Waiting at the Water's Edge was first performed at the Bush Theatre on January 5th, 1993 with the following cast:

Cast

Violet Evans
(15, from South Wales)............................Suzanna Hamilton
Susie Owen
(15, from North Wales)...............................Helen Anderson
Therese Couth
(40, French, living in England).....................Amelda Brown
Will Couth
(20, her son)...Christopher Eccleston
Davie Maclean
(from Nova Scotia)..Callum Dixon

Director...Polly Teale
Producer.............Kate Danielson for Pangloss Productions
Designer...Alice Purcell

The action takes place between November 1923 and June 1925, in Harlech (North Wales), Richmond (London), and New Waterford (Nova Scotia). Dialogue in brackets ( ) is spoken in Welsh.

Act One
SCENE ONE

[Two young women sit apart on a deserted beach. It is dry, but cold, with a strong wind. Their coats are fastened against the weather. Vi sits staring out to the horizon. Su sits watching her. Vi looks at Su, then back to the horizon. Su watches her even more intently.]

VI: Wanna picture?

SU: Own the beach then, do you?

VI: No.

SU: Well then.

[Vi goes back to watching.]

I saw you from the top road.

[Su moves slightly closer.]

VI: Don't you know it's rude to stare?

SU: I'm not staring.

VI: No?

SU: I'm watching.

VI: What's the difference?

SU: Staring's rude.

VI: And watching's not?

SU: Watching's how you learn.

[Vi resumes her look-out.]

SU: You were here yesterday. *[No response.]* I nearly

9

come down then, but it was too blowy. My mam said I'd get blown away nigh on. She said you must be daft or something. (What d'you think of that?)

VI: I don't answer to Welsh.

SU: Might've been talkin' to myself.

VI: First sign of madness.

SU: NO! I thought lookin' for the hairs on the palm of your hand.

VI: That's the second sign.

[Sue checks her palms.]

SU: Nothing there. I must be in the early stages.

[Vi gets up. Moves about six inches away. Sits down. Su moves six inches after her. Vi is furious.]

VI: Why can't you just go away?

SU: Go where?

VI: I don't know. Anywhere.

SU: I like it here.

VI: There are five and a half miles of sandy beach at Harlech. So what are you doin' sittin' almost up my nose?

SU: Keepin' you company?

[Vi gets up.]

VI: Why don't you just clear off to the other side of the bay?

[Su looks in that direction. It is empty.]

SU: 'Cos then I'd be by myself.

[Vi gives up and sits down.]

Can I stay then?

[Vi shrugs.]

Thanks.

[Vi stares out to the horizon.]

Could I ask you something?

VI: No.

SU: You're not a very friendly person.

VI: Can't you see I'm busy?

SU: What're you doin'?

VI: I'm waitin'.

SU: Waiting for who then?

VI: For the sun.

SU: What son?

VI: THE sun. THE sun. The sun in the sky.

SU: Well you won't be gettin' burnt today will you?

[Vi puts her hands over her ears. Suddenly it goes dark as a cloud cuts across the sun. Vi's hands fall from her ears. Su looks up.]

VI: Black cloud.

SU: Bad luck.

[Vi concentrates hard.]

VI: No.

SU: Means something.

VI: Yes. But not what...you...think!

[The sun is revealed again. Vi is relieved. Su is impressed.]

SU: There. You can see it again now.

VI: Yes.

SU: And it can see us maybe.

VI: Maybe.

SU: Well. There it is then. The sun. THE sun. The sun in the sky.

VI: Not for long.

SU: *[worried]* Why?

VI: It's going to set soon.

SU: Oh. What's your name?

VI: Vi.

         [Su waits.]

         What's yours?

SU: Su. But my mam calls me Susie.

VI: Susie.

SU: You could come to my house for tea if you liked.

VI: No thanks.

SU: Oh.

VI: I promised my aunt I'd get back.

SU: Who's your aunt then?

VI: Mrs Williams on the top road.

SU: Hey! My mam knows her. We know her really well. Maybe my mam could ask her if you could come to tea tomorrow.

VI: P'raps.

SU: Would you like that?

VI: I don't know.

SU: I could run home now and ask.

VI: If you like.

SU: Okay — I won't be long.

[Su is about to leave. Then —]

You'll still be here when I get back?

VI: Maybe.

SU: Couldn't you wait for me?

VI: No. No, I couldn't. What *is* the matter with you?

SU: I'm lonely.

VI: I'm not surprised.

SU: Why are you being like this?

VI: Because I'm busy.

SU: You're not busy. You're just staring.

VI: I'm waiting for the sun to set.

SU: But why?

VI: Because... because sometimes things have a meaning.

SU: What — like black clouds bring bad luck?

VI: No. That's just stupid. Not a meaning that's always there. One that only comes at the right time. To the right person.

[Vi looks out at the horizon. Su is confused. She wanders away and begins to pick things up from the sand. She then gradually turns her attention back to the sun.]

SU: Not long now.

VI: No.

SU: I like Mrs Williams. You staying long with her?

[Vi shrugs.]

Where're you from?

VI: Senghennydd.

[Sue's face falls.]

SU: Oh. What's it like there now?

VI: It's just a place.

SU: I s'pose.

VI: Anyway, I'm going away soon.

SU: I couldn't stay in a place like that.

VI: Like what?

SU: Where something had happened. All those men. Dead.

VI: I'm going to England.

SU: Hey! So am I. And marry a rich man and bring him home.

VI: Once you've gone, you can't come back.

SU: Why not?

VI: You just can't.

SU: Well, I shall.

VI: Not me. Never in a million years.

[Su lifts her coat and dress to reveal an underskirt.]

SU: See this? Made out of Lady Gladys Fotheray's nightdress. My mam takes in their laundry.

VI: Very grand.

SU: She said to my mam, she said, "Here, Mrs Owen — a little something for your Susan". Lucky I've only brothers. You got any brothers?

[Vi shakes her head.]

Sisters?

VI: No.

[Silence.]

SU: Did you hear it, the explosion?

VI: 'Course I did.

SU: Thing like that you'd never forget.

VI: I was only little.

SU: Still....

VI: The windows shook. Then a terrible bang. And for a while bells, ringing the alarm, and people running everywhere. Then nothing. Quiet. The smell of burning. And the next day, the field black with people come from all the valleys to see what had happened.

SU: Your da... he wasn't...?

VI: My father started in the mine when he was twelve. The seam was only twenty-six inches high. He said you were exhausted by the time you got there. He said his trousers would stand up by themselves with the sweat. That morning, he came down as usual. He had a routine, you see. Sat in the same chair. Smoked one cigarette lit with one match. Like magic it was. Real magic. Strong. Then this morning, he sat down and he said it felt cold as the grave. It just struck cold like never before, the chair. And he went to light his cigarette, but before it caught, the match went out. He put on his coat and set off. Got halfway out our back gate, and came back. He stayed home that day. And two hours later it went up.

SU: No!

VI: We watched them from the field, my mam and me. Bringing up the bodies. As many as five to a house there were. And we watched my da. Carrying them home.

SU: But your da knew.

VI: He knew something. He received a message, you

see. That's why I say things don't always have a meaning. A chair and a match. They don't mean much normally, do they?

SU: Nothing.

VI: But that day, they did.

SU: But why didn'e tell 'em? Why didn'e warn 'em?

VI: He didn't know for sure. Not till it happened.

SU: That's terrible.

VI: And my da never went back down.

SU: Doesn't bear thinkin' about.

VI: Never.

SU: What did he do after?

VI: He had special work.

SU: Oh.

VI: Watchin' out for things. I helped him.

SU: I see. *[pause]* It couldn't have been a coincidence, could it?

VI: Coincidence?

SU: What happened.

VI: The chair *and* the match.

SU: No. That's terrible. He still do his special work?

VI: He's dead.

SU: Sorry.

VI: Last week with his lungs.

SU: Oh.

VI: In the night. You'd think you'd feel something, but you don't.

SU: No?

16

VI: I didn't know till morning.

SU: And your mam?

VI: Woke up 'cos she couldn't hear 'im breathing any more. Used to say the noise kept her awake. Now she can't sleep for the quiet. Cries all the time. That's why I'm staying with my aunt.

SU: Oh.

[Su looks out at the setting sun.]

Nearly there. What d'you think it'll tell you?

VI: Dunno.

SU: What if you don't see it?

VI: If I don't see it, it won't be there.

SU: Had I better go after all?

[Vi thinks, shrugs. Su settles down and gathers the courage to ask Vi something.]

Vi? Will I see the meaning?

VI: Maybe. Maybe you'll see it and I won't. Maybe neither.

SU: Maybe both.

VI: I don't think so.

[Su sits away from Vi. She composes herself suitably for someone about to receive a meaning. After a while she speaks.]

SU: Why d'you want a meanin', Vi?

VI: I don't know. So I won't be always alone.

[Su considers this.]

SU: I'm alone since my friend Megan got a boyfriend.

VI: Sh!

[Vi raises her hand to silence Su. They both watch,

transfixed, as the sun disappears very slowly below the horizon. Silence. When the sun is gone, Vi is disappointed, empty. Su is carried away.]

Oh well. I've got to the end of the week.

SU: You didn't feel anything?

VI: It's not what you feel, it's what you receive.

SU: Well, I didn't receive anything, but I feel fantastic!

VI: I should go now.

[Vi gets up. Su jumps up to follow her.]

SU: What will you do if you don't get a message before the end of the week?

VI: I'll have to look somewhere else.

SU: Where?

VI: I've got to get off.

SU: See you tomorrow then.

VI: Maybe.

SU: Ask your aunt if you can come to tea with me. Su. Susie Owen.

VI: I'll see.

SU: Why've you gone funny again?

VI: You make me talk too much.

[Vi walks away, into the distance.]

SU: I'll be quiet tomorrow. Honest. I'll be quiet. Only ask your aunt, why don't you? *[calls after her]* Su. Susie Owen. Don't forget me.

[Su watches as Vi disappears into the distance. Then she looks back to the sunset and feels the magic of it again, drinks it in.]

SCENE TWO

[The drawing room of the Couth's house, Richmond. Night. Therese sits at an embroidery frame on which is stretched a piece of fine white linen. She works the embroidery with her left hand although she is right-handed. She has been waiting a long time. There is a knock at the door and Su enters.]

THERESE: Yes?

SU: I was just wonderin', mum. Will there be anything else?

THERESE: My son's room is ready?

SU: Yes, mum.

THERESE: A good fire?

SU: Stoked to the nines, mum.

THERESE: Tell the new girl to turn down the bed.

SU: Mum.

THERESE: Is there word from Mary?

SU: Dress fitting's Thursday. She's back first thing Friday. You'll miss 'er when she's married.

THERESE: Indeed. It is to her lasting credit that in the seven years she has worked for me I have never once noticed her. You could learn a great deal from her example.

[Su stares her out briefly, bobs a resentful curtsey and leaves. Therese sinks, regards her work with despair. Outside, the doorbell rings. Therese collects herself, arranges her dress, returns to her embroidery. Su bursts through the door, knocking as she enters, a telegram in her outstretched hand. Therese is appalled.]

THERESE: What is this?

SU: Telegram, mum.

19

THERESE: You never pass anything from your hand to mine. That is the purpose of the salver in the hall. And when you touch the salver, you do so wearing gloves. Is that understood?

SU: Yes.

THERESE: Yes what?

SU: Yes.... thank you.

[Therese takes the telegram, reads it, folds it up and puts it away. She sits rigid. Su clears her throat.]

THERESE: Get out.

[Su leaves. Therese breathes and returns to her embroidery. The doorbell rings again. She pauses, then continues. After a few seconds, Will enters. Therese sews on.]

WILL: I'm late.

THERESE: So you are.

WILL: How will you ever forgive me?

[Therese catches a thread from the work.]

THERESE: Perhaps you could pass me my scissors.

WILL: Of course.

[He goes to pass them, sees the stiffness in her hand and cuts the thread himself.]

Any more?

THERESE: That's fine. Thank you.

WILL: A devil of a journey.

[Therese struggles to re-thread her needle.]

I could do that.

THERESE: No need.

WILL: But it would be so easy for me....

THERESE: Very tactful, William.

WILL: I'm sorry. I didn't mean to be....

THERESE: Cruel?

WILL: Is that what I was?

[Therese shrugs.]

I'm sorry. You don't seem very pleased to see me.

THERESE: Here are the two of us in a large room. High ceilings. Long windows. And yet, the room feels cramped. All the months here alone, it feels so empty. But now you are here, and it is unbearably cramped. I've been too long alone.

WILL: I got a letter saying not to come.

[Therese huffs. She is bitter.]

You wanted me to concentrate on my exams.

[She returns to her work.]

So.

THERESE: "So"?

WILL: So it isn't my fault.

THERESE: It is my fault then?

WILL: I don't say it's anyone's fault. I just... thought... I don't know what you want me to say. Can I start again?

THERESE: Such luxury.

WILL: I'm sorry I'm late. I bumped into someone. We got talking. You know how the time....

THERESE: Yes, I know how time....

[She gives him the telegram.]

From your father. Delayed on business. Exquisite manners, your father. No word from him for six

21

months, and he declines a dinner invitation with "delayed on business". I thought he might have made an effort for tonight. You are his son, after all.

WILL: It doesn't matter.

THERESE: You see how we never learn from experience. Do you remember when I fell from a horse and broke my ankle? The doctor said "Well, that will teach you not to fall off horses." Such is the value of experience. It makes us old and teaches us nothing. He wept when you were born.

WILL: You told me.

THERESE: It's important to remember.

WILL: But it's more important to forget.

THERESE: To forget? That requires forward motion. A present to displace the past. I have no such present.

WILL: But you will have.

THERESE: I don't think so.

WILL: Of course. You'll get well.

THERESE: No.

WILL: It's bound to take time. We have to be patient.

THERESE: We?

WILL: You.

THERESE: Yes. You're leaving soon.

WILL: I've only just arrived.

THERESE: But you are going away again. Tell me.

WILL: We can talk about this later.

THERESE: Tell me now. I will not be deserted by degrees. Not this time.

WILL: You know I wouldn't do that.

THERESE: If you were coming home to stay you would have been here on time. And you wouldn't hold yourself apart, polite, afraid even to touch me.

WILL: No.

THERESE: Is it far?

WILL: Yes.

THERESE: Be careful, William. Travelling between places weakens a person. Look at me. I should never have left France. My family. Here I have no one.

           [Silence.]

WILL: The man I was talking to, he's been working in Canada. There's a lot going on out there at the moment. A lot closing down but new opportunities opening up too. It's all change. And it's a place where a man could get the measure of himself.

           [Therese looks around her.]

           Ma?

THERESE: Oh, I'm sorry dear, I thought your father must have come in, you sound so like him. And he does have interests in Canada, doesn't he?

WILL: Yes. Yes, he does.

THERESE: Timber. Mining. Am I getting close?

WILL: It's an opportunity for me. It's a chance for me to see what I can do. To find out who I am.

THERESE: I only hope you won't be disappointed.

           [Will roars in frustration and anger.]

WILL: This isn't how I wanted it to be.

THERESE: No. You wanted me to make it easy for you.

WILL: I wanted to explain.

THERESE: Explain?

WILL: That I'd send for you.

THERESE: Send for me?

WILL: Once I'm set up.

THERESE: Come to Canada?

WILL: Why not?

THERESE: And what would I do in Canada? Embroider pillowslips, perhaps? Give tea parties?

WILL: If that's what you wanted.

THERESE: What I wanted? Let us not speak now of what I wanted. All this talk of "what I wanted" has puckered the linen. The stitches are too tight.

WILL: I'm sorry.

THERESE: My therapy. What do you think of my therapy?

WILL: It's lovely.

THERESE: Lovely?

WILL: Yes. It makes me feel....

[She tips the frame. It clatters to the floor.]

THERESE: Now, William. You were telling me about your feelings.

WILL: Sad. It makes me feel sad.

THERESE: Don't cultivate your sensitivity, William. You never know where it might lead. Before you know it, you're like a wireless anyone can tune into. Full of indecision. No use at all in Canada. You and your father have lovely manners, William. And that boyish charm. Stick with them.

WILL: I am not him.

[He goes to pick up the frame.]

THERESE: Don't touch that. Ring for the maid.

[*He continues. Therese shouts.*]

I said ring for the maid!

[*Will drops the frame.*]

WILL: Ring for her yourself.

[*Therese struggles to her feet and crosses the room painfully.*]

THERESE: You think I can't, is that right? I am a useless old woman who cannot even run her own home, and you are a big man, yes?

[*She rings the bell and picks up a small wooden box.*]

Well since you are a man, now, all of a sudden, it is not for me to keep your toys.

[*She hurls the contents of the box at him. Marbles, tin soldiers, a tiny marionette and a magnet fall to the floor. Will picks them up. He has not seen them in years.*]

What a fool I've been. Keeping these for you. Using my life for a museum. I want you to go away. Just go away. You're going sooner or later so it might as well be now. You shouldn't have come. You should not have come. I thought you wouldn't come. I thought you'd never come.

[*Therese can barely support herself. Will goes to hold her.*]

Don't touch me, please don't touch me. Not if you're going away.

[*He clasps her.*]

Not if you're going away.

WILL: Forgive me, forgive me. I'm not going anywhere.

THERESE: Please don't lie to me.

WILL: It's just an idea. It may never happen. I'll probably

never go. Sit down now.

[He sits her down. She struggles to collect herself. Will rights the frame. There is a knock and Su enters.]

WILL: Yes. Could you bring us two glasses? There's a bottle of Eau de Vie in my smallest case there.

SU: Sir.

[Su bobs and leaves. Will kneels beside his mother and holds her hands.]

THERESE: Eau de Vie.

WILL: You see, I'm not all bad. I should have come. You should have made me come.

THERESE: My fault again?

WILL: No. But look at you. Look at you.

THERESE: Sh, now. I am making progress. Making pillow-slips.

WILL: I am sorry.

THERESE: Sh.

WILL: It is lovely.

THERESE: It was to be finished for when you came home, but...

[She shrugs. He hugs her. There is a knock and Su enters with two very large tumblers and a bottle of Mirabeille on a tray. She wears white cotton gloves. Will rushes to take the tray from her.]

WILL: Well, they're good big glasses.

SU: Oh yes, sir.

WILL: We won't be wanting anything else now.

SU: Okay-dokey.

[Su bobs and leaves. Will shows the glasses to Therese.]

THERESE: You should call her back and make her change them.

WILL: She must have thought we'd be needing plenty.

[He pours two tots and hands Therese a glass.]

Salut.

[They drink.]

THERESE: I'm sorry about the box. Is anything broken?

[Will fetches the magnet.]

WILL: Everything's fine. I'll show you a trick. Give me a needle.

[She does so. He magnetises it.]

THERESE: Does it still pull?

[He nods. He pushes it through a cork.]

WILL: I didn't know you'd kept these things.

[She shrugs. He drops the cork into her glass.]

There. The needle will always point North. So if I ever go away — if — you'll know how to find me.

SCENE THREE

[An attic room in the Couth's house. Two poor beds. A skylight. Vi lies on her bed looking at a book. Su enters, pulling off her uniform.]

SU: I'm so blummin' tired, I could drop like a stone. I'm serious. Up and down, up and down like a yo-yo. The sooner Mary's back and you're trained the better. I don't know how she stands it. I don't know how you'll stand it.

VI: I'll stand it.

SU: When you're with them it's like you don't exist.

VI: It won't bother me.

SU: You've got to be a saint. It's gloves now, she wants. Gloves. I'd rather spend the next year in that kitchen sandin' those pans till my hands're drippin' blood than put up with all that. I truly would. You don't know what you're lettin' yourself in for. Now there's two of 'em!

VI: Don't upset yourself.

SU: Fetch and do.

[Su wriggles into her nightie.]

All that fuss and bother over nothing. You know, when I come 'ere I thought they'd be really... you know, refined. Like the Fotherays. Giving parties and dances and people comin' and goin' all the time. But they're not refined. They're just picky. You'd never credit what goes on. Today, she said to me, she said, "Is this your idea of a fruit knife?" I mean the way she said it. I nearly said "I don't have ideas about fruit knives. I'm too busy for havin' ideas about fruit knives." My idea of a fruit knife. I should've said "Well it blummin' well cuts, doesn't it?" My idea. Never again. They only have fruit knives so you and me can get 'em wrong. So we can't keep up. That's why she's rich and I'm not. "Fruit knife?" I nearly said, "Well, it's only an apple so I'll wipe it on my pinny and you can stick it straight in your gob." But you can't, can you?

[Su gets into bed and snuggles up.]

I'm all het up now.

[Silence.]

SU: You're readin' then?

VI: That's right.

SU: What's your book?

VI: It's just pictures.

SU: What they of then, the pictures?

        [Vi shows her the cover.]

        Lives of the Saints? Am I in? I should be.

VI: No.

        [Su hauls herself out of bed and sits near Vi.]

        I thought you were tired.

SU: Too tired to sleep.

        [Vi continues to look at the book, allowing Su to see the pictures.]

        Sorry I went on a bit.

        [Vi shrugs. Su looks at the book.]

VI: What d'you want, Su?

SU: Just bein' friendly.

VI: Really?

SU: What's wrong with that?

VI: Nothing.

SU: But that book's too depressing for me.

VI: Don't look if it upsets you.

        [Vi snaps the book shut. She takes out her boots from under the bed.]

SU: Now I'll never sleep I shouldn't think.

VI: You'll drop off in no time. You always do.

SU: How d'you know?

VI: Well how d'you think?

SU: I might just have my eyes closed and be restin'!

VI: What d'you want, Su?

SU: I give up with you.

VI: Good. Now go to bed.

[Vi scrubs away at her boots with a brush. Su sits on the end of her own bed.]

SU: You got your letter then, did you?

VI: Yes, thank you.

SU: That's nice, a letter.

VI: Yes.

SU: Who's it from then?

VI: Never you mind.

SU: Go on.

VI: No.

SU: Why not?

VI: None of your business.

SU: Please.

VI: I don't know.

SU: You don't know who it's from?

VI: No.

SU: Haven't you opened it?

VI: No.

SU: Why not?

VI: I'm savin' it.

SU: What for?

VI: I'm waitin' for the right time.

SU: And you don't even know who it's from?

VI: No.

SU: Well, it's not from your mam, I'll tell you that for nothing.

VI: How d'you know that?

SU: It was posted in Rhydyfelan. What would your mam be doin' there?

VI: How d'you know where it was posted?

SU: 'Cos I looked.

VI: Can I not have anything to myself? Am I allowed no privacy whatsoever?

SU: How many letters do we get here in a month, eh? Answer me that.

VI: I don't know.

SU: Two maybe. And that's including cook. And then you come along, and you've not been here two minutes when a letter arrives.

VI: It's not the point.

SU: I'm only human, that's the point. I'm sorry, Vi, but I'm only flesh and blood, and if I see a letter, I can't help but wonder. I didn' open it or nothin'.

VI: And I'm to be grateful for that, I suppose?

SU: Well, I'm sorry. I never thought you'd be so upset.

[Vi takes the letter from inside her slip. She studies it.]

VI: *[to herself]* Rhydyfelan.

SU: I bet you anything you don't dare open it 'cos you think it's bad news. I bet it's from someone really important and you're scared in case it's bad news.

VI: Don't be stupid.

SU: What if it's really urgent, and by not opening it you'll never know and some tragically sad event will take place.

VI: It's from a man.

SU: I knew. I bet it says "Dear Violet..." I bet that's how it starts. Don't you want to know? How can you bear it?

VI: I can bear it.

SU: It's unnatural.

VI: I can't read.

        [Silence.]

SU: Can't read? Don't be daft. What d'you mean you can't read? Can't read Miss Cleverclogs!

VI: I can't read.

SU: Your aunty told me you won a prize once for sayin' a poem.

VI: What else did she tell you?

SU: Nothing.

VI: No?

SU: No.

VI: I learnt it, that poem.

SU: Learnt it? The whole thing?

VI: By heart. I'm good at learnin'.

SU: You can't read. You couldn't even read Rhydyfelan.

VI: Sometimes I can read a bit but the letters go backwards and forwards so sometimes I can't read my own name.

SU: Violet Evans cannot read.

        [Vi holds out the letter for Su to read.]

        I couldn't.

VI: 'Course you could.

SU: Really.

32

VI: Just read it Su, then bed.

                [Su takes the letter and opens it.]

SU: Okay. Ready? "Dear Violet..." Didn't I tell you! Didn't I say that's how it would start?

VI: Give it here.

                [Su hands over the letter. Vi looks at it, folds it, puts it back inside her shirt.]

                That's all I need to know.

SU: What?

                [Vi goes back to her book.]

VI: I can guess the rest.

                [Su's mouth opens very wide. Lost for words, she gets into her bed. Silence.]

SU: Just so long as we know.

VI: Know what?

SU: That this is how it's going to be.

                [Vi goes back to her book.]

                Just so long as we know.

                [Su turns her back. Tries to sleep. After a while, her breathing changes. Vi puts away the book. She then whispers:]

VI: Su? Susie?

                [No response. Vi opens her suitcase, takes out a man's overcoat. She puts it on, tucking her hair down the back. She then pulls on a flat cap. Su looks up.]

SU: What're you on with?

                [Vi jumps.]

VI: Sh! Keep your voice down.

SU: Where did you get that?

VI: It was my da's.

SU: Well, what's it doin' here?

VI: I've got to go now.

SU: You're mad. D'you want to get the chop?

VI: It's alright. I do it all the time.

SU: You're joking.

VI: It's alright. I promise.

SU: Where d'you go?

VI: The river. But not for long.

SU: In the middle of the night?

VI: Yes.

SU: Who with?

VI: Nobody.

SU: You must think I'm thick.

VI: Honest, Su. Cross my heart.

SU: How d'you get out?

VI: Through the pantry window round the back.

SU: You leave the window open?

VI: Yes.

SU: And I'm up here in my own in bed? Don't you care what might happen to me?

VI: Nothing's happened so far has it?

SU: And what does that prove? That I've been lucky.

VI: Don't be daft. I'm only gone ten minutes.

SU: You're gonna get the sack and I'm glad 'cos you're mental. You're a danger to yourself and others.

VI: I'm not scared.

SU: Well, you should be.

VI: In this get-up? Who's going to bother me?

SU: Vi! Don't go. What if something happens and they ask me?

VI: Say you were asleep.

SU: Vi! Don't go.

VI: I've got to. Or I'm gonna be late.

SU: For what?

VI: Midnight. I like to hear the bells.

[Su shuts up.]

See you in the morning.

[No response.]

Su?

[Nothing.]

What's wrong? *[pause]* You've gone all quiet. *[pause]* I can't stand it here caged up. I've got to get some air.

SU: So open the skylight.

VI: I like the boats.

SU: You're obsessed.

VI: I have to be ready.

SU: For what?

VI: *[begins reluctantly]* Some days you look out at the sea and it's blue. Yeah? Some days you look out at the sea and it's grey. Or it's black or it's white, or it's green like a starling. But one day, you look at the sea, and it's waiting.

[Pause.]

VI: I have to go now.

SU: I don't like it.

VI: I know that.

SU: Watch out, then.

VI: Night.

SCENE FOUR

[A bridge overlooking the Thames. Lights on the water. A clear night. Vi leans against the rail. Below, in the Couth's kitchen, Will sits drinking. Vi holds the envelope containing her letter at arm's length and guesses at its contents.]

VI: Dear Violet. Dear Violet. Dear Violet...

[She presses the envelope against her forehead and hesitates.]

Dear Violet... You're a good girl... you know that... a girl your da would be proud of. Which brings me to your mam. Your mam... *[she falters, then resumes]* She's stopped crying now, and she has plenty of friends. Not like before. Your Aunty Kitty has her over every Sunday after Chapel. You have nothing to be ashamed of. You have your da's work to get on with. I know it isn't always easy, but we cannot change the hand we have been given. Don't feel bad about leaving. You had to get away. I understand. So keep on going and never look back would be my motto. Your loving uncle — Ellis.

[Vi looks at the envelope, satisfied. She puts it away. She leaves the bridge. Below, Will is pacing the kitchen, changing direction with wild unpredictability, testing the compass in his glass. Violet slips in and surprises both of them.]

WILL: Who the hell?

[Violet pulls off her cap.]

VI:	Hello.
WILL:	Who are you?
VI:	I work here.
WILL:	Work here?
VI:	Parlour maid. Soon as Mary's married.
WILL:	Where've you been?
VI:	Out. Am I to get the chop now?
WILL:	The what?
VI:	The sack. Am I to be given the sack?
WILL:	No. No, of course not.
VI:	Well thank you, sir. Goodnight.

[Vi makes to leave.]

WILL:	Whoa, whoa, whoa.
VI:	Sir?
WILL:	You know who I am?
VI:	You're Mrs Couth's son, I think.
WILL:	Yes. I was wondering... where've you been?
VI:	By the river.
WILL:	Courting.
VI:	No, sir. Not courting. I just wanted to get some air, so if that's all, sir...
WILL:	It's not. There's this. *[he shows her the glass]* Here, try it.

[He pushes the glass into her hands.]

WILL:	Follow the needle.

[Vi takes a couple of steps.]

VI:	Very nice.

WILL: No, you have to walk all around, change direction to get the full effect.

[Vi walks around. The needle turns. She is impressed.]

VI: It's magnetised.

[He takes the magnet from his pocket and holds it out to her. She has to go to him to take it. She hesitates, then moves, takes the magnet, and pulls away again. Vi turns it over in her hand.]

VI: It's good.

WILL: I'm glad you like it.

VI: I have to go now.

[She puts it down.]

WILL: Many boats on the river?

VI: Some.

WILL: Fabulous things, boats. Full of hope. And from here — you could go anywhere, you know. Africa, Norway, Turkey. Along the waterways.

VI: My da built boats.

WILL: Amazing! What sort?

VI: Small ones.

WILL: Sea-faring?

VI: We didn't live near the sea, so he never got to try them out.

WILL: Oh. Toy boats.

VI: No. Real boats, they were. Proper boats. Strong.

WILL: A hobby.

VI: No. Not a hobby. It was later on, after things changed. More than a hobby. It was special work he had to do. I helped him.

WILL: But they never got near the water?

VI: No.

WILL: Frustrating!

VI: I s'pose.

WILL: So where are they now?

VI: They're not. They got smashed up. For wood.

WILL: That's a shame.

VI: My mam. She never liked them. *[pause]* I should be off now.

WILL: I'm going on a ship soon.

VI: Oh?

WILL: To Nova Scotia.

VI: Nova Scotia?

WILL: Canada. Just off the East coast.

VI: Is it far?

WILL: Very.

VI: How far?

WILL: Way over the Atlantic. An amazing place. Huge, huge skies. Fabulous coastline. As much air as you like there.

VI: You've been before?

WILL: No. Somebody told me.

VI: Why're you going?

WILL: My father. He has a stake in a company out there. Coal and Power. It's had its day I'm afraid. We want out. Cut our losses. Trouble is they've got some dispute on.

VI: A dispute?

WILL: Strike. Miners.

VI: Why're they striking?

WILL: Boom's been and gone. We can import twice what we want for half what it costs to produce it. We've had no choice but to cut wages. Anyway, it's got to be settled.

VI: How?

WILL: How?... Well, take the necessary measures.

VI: Like what?

WILL: Whatever's appropriate.

VI: Starve them out?

WILL: I doubt it'll come to that.

VI: It might.

WILL: I hope not.

VI: Could you do it?

WILL: I could do whatever had to be done.

VI: Have you done it before?

WILL: No. No, I haven't.

VI: So how will you know, about what to do?

WILL: We shouldn't talk about it. It's depressing.

VI: We shouldn't talk at all.

WILL: No.

VI: I should probably go now.

            [Will rushes to find something in his jacket pocket.]

WILL: I have my ticket here.

            [He holds it out to her. She takes it and reads it over again and again.]

            I thought I might throw a party before I went.

Perhaps you'll be there... I'm sorry, I don't know your name.

VI: Violet.

[She returns the ticket.]

WILL: I thought if I sent out invitations it might keep me from changing my mind.

VI: Why would you want to do that?

WILL: A million reasons.

VI: Will you know people in Nova Scotia?

WILL: No.

VI: And they won't know you? Know anything about you?

WILL: Only what I tell them.

VI: You should go. A place like that. You're lucky. I'd go.

WILL: I'm being sent as a test. See if I sink or swim.

VI: Isn't it worth it for the chance, though?

WILL: That's what I'll find out.

VI: I have to be off now.

[Pause.]

WILL: D'you think this really happened, Violet?

VI: Sir?

WILL: D'you think I really followed this compass in my glass and met a parlour maid dressed as a man whose father built boats miles away from the sea?

VI: I don't know, sir.

WILL: If you gave me something, I could be sure.

VI: I don't have anything.

WILL: I'd be prepared to give you something too....

[Will goes through his pockets, turning them out.]

There must be something, and then we would know....

VI: Your magnet.

WILL: This?

VI: Yes.

WILL: Okay.

[He holds the magnet up. Vi tugs at the bottom of her blouse.]

VI: I would give you this button. *[she tears it free]* Mother of pearl.

[They exchange.]

WILL: So in the morning we'll find out.

VI: Yes.

WILL: Goodnight, Violet.

VI: Goodnight, Sir.

[She goes to leave.]

WILL: Violet — *[Vi is gone]* it's been a pleasure.

SCENE FIVE

[The Couth's kitchen. Vi washes her hair in a bucket. Su watches. She is nervous and quiet.]

SU: You shouldn't do that.

VI: Old wife.

SU: Not when it's your time.

VI: Stupid stories.

[Silence.]

42

SU: Please, Vi. We got enough on with Mary.

VI: Scared I'll go mad're you?

SU: Why not? I know a girl did. All the bad blood run to 'er 'ead it did, doin' just what you are now.

VI: Listenin' t'you prob'ly turned 'er brain.

SU: Vi, don't! Poor Mary. I've had t'pack up all her things.

VI: You'll get over it.

SU: She liked you, y'know.

VI: Did she?

SU: Said you knew how to fit in. Walk quiet-like. She's right too. Like a ghost about the place.

VI: She'll be alright, Su.

        [Vi wraps a towel around her hair.]

SU: How d'you know?

VI: I just do.

SU: Gotta message about it, did you?

VI: No.

SU: Well then. *[pause]* Cook says it was knitting needles she tried it with. Pints and pints o'blood there was.

VI: Nasty gossip.

SU: I didn't even know she was... you know.

VI: You'd've helped her be rid of it then, would you?

SU: Would you?

VI: Maybe.

SU: I really thought she was gettin' married.

VI: Just get on with something. Take your mind off it.

43

SU: How can I settle?

VI: Try.

SU: You're as bad as them upstairs, you are. I might as well not be here.

VI: Don't get my hopes up if you're stopping. *[Su turns away]* Sorry.

SU: You're hard, you are.

VI: I said sorry.

SU: Hard as nails.

VI: Good.

SU: You've always been the same.

VI: Have I, indeed?

SU: That's what my mam says.

VI: Your mam?

SU: She says there's something wrong with you. She asked your aunt.

VI: She did what?

SU: When I told my mam you was comin' to work here she said to me "You wanna watch yourself Susie, that girl's got no friends."

VI: That's a lie.

SU: "You've got to feel sorry for her but there's no smoke without fire."

VI: Big mouth mam.

SU: No, she's not....

VI: Wouldn't know the truth if it bit her.

SU: "No friends now and never did. Not since the mine went up."

VI: Wrong. Stupid. Big mouth mam.

SU: "There's something black and hard inside of her."

VI: I'm glad that's what your mam says, I'm glad, it makes me laugh, haha...

SU: "And ever since then...."

VI: I'm glad, I'm glad, you're just like all the rest....

SU: "And ever since then her dad went strange and she went with him."

VI: No! My da was special!

SU: Your da went mad in his head! Thought he was Noah, building boats!

[Vi slaps Su hard in the face. They are both completely shocked by it. Silence.]

VI: I'm sorry, Su. Let me see.

[Su pulls away.]

SU: I only wanted to be your friend.

VI: I didn't mean to....

[She pulls away again.]

It just happened. *[no response]* Does it hurt? I....

[Su isn't listening. Vi pulls away, towels her hair and starts to comb it. There is a long silence while Su collects herself.]

SU: I'm sorry. About what I said.

VI: I hope Mary gets better.

SU: Might want her job back if she does. *[Vi shrugs]* I could do that for you.

VI: It's nearly finished.

SU: Go on.

[Vi hesitates, then holds out the comb. Su takes it and starts to comb Vi's hair very gently. After a few

seconds, she puts her arms round Vi's shoulders, hugs her and releases her. Vi takes back the comb.]

You got nice hair.

VI: I'm gonna cut it all off one day.

SU: You're always sayin' that, but you never do.

VI: Really short. Right up the back, like a boy.

[Vi lifts her hair.]

SU: You've got a lovely neck. Like a swan.

[Vi bears it for as long as she can, then picks up her bucket and goes off, leaving Su watching after her.]

SCENE SIX

[Vi stands on the bridge. She wears her father's coat and cap. Church bells strike midnight. The wind is high. Vi squeezes the envelope in her fist, holds it up to the river and shouts, agitated.]

VI: Dear Violet... Dear Violet. Do not worry about your mam. Only try to hold steady. You know what other people are, so stay away from them. They are ignorant and stupid and not worth the bothering with. They will punish you forever if you let them, and you are not to blame. You don't need them. You mustn't need them. One day you will show them and then they'll be sorry. They will be sorry. And your mam will be sorry to. When she sees he was special. As you are yourself. You are special, Vi. Never ever forget that. *[she calms herself, and thinks]* Watch out for yourself, and get a move on where they don't know you. Keep moving, Vi, and never look back. Your only uncle, your father's brother, Ellis.

[She steadies herself, breathing hard, clutching the letter to her. Will calls as he walks onto the bridge.]

46

WILL: Hello!

[Vi jumps.]

VI: Were you listening?

WILL: I wouldn't eavesdrop on a secret letter.

VI: It's not secret.

WILL: No?

VI: It's from my uncle.

WILL: Ah.

VI: So that's a disappointment for you.

WILL: Is it?

VI: I'd say so.

WILL: And why's that?

VI: Because it's not what you thought.

WILL: And what did I think?

VI: That it was from a man.

WILL: And so it is.

VI: A different sort of man.

WILL: How many sorts are there?

VI: A lover.

WILL: I have your button here.

VI: You can keep it.

WILL: Perhaps I'll sew it on the bottom of my shirt.

VI: Your shirt?

WILL: Why not?

[Vi shrugs, then says:]

VI: Would you wear it to go to Nova Scotia?

WILL: Well not every day. It's quite a long journey. *[Vi is not laughing]* Tell you what. I'll put it on a thread. Wear it round my neck. How's that?

VI: That's... thank you. Thanks.

WILL: You're enough to make me wish I wasn't going.

VI: I wouldn't stop you.

WILL: It's a shame you can't go with me.

VI: It's a shame I can't go instead of you.

WILL: Charming.

VI: I don't mean to be rude. But I have my reasons.

WILL: And what are they, Vi?

VI: Secret.

WILL: And better than mine, I imagine. I'm only going so I don't have to stay. But then I'd only stay because I'm scared of leaving.

VI: Scared of leaving?

WILL: Of what will happen to my mother. I lied to her, told her it was just an idea.

VI: She's sick.

WILL: Yes.

VI: Will she get better?

WILL: I think so.

VI: Well then.

WILL: She'll be alone.

VI: She's alone now.

WILL: But if I stayed, I could change that.

VI: Could you?

WILL: Maybe not.

VI: Don't look back.

WILL: That's what my father says.

VI: He's right.

WILL: But he's not very nice.

VI: It's the only way.

WILL: I don't think I'm up to it.

VI: Tell her tonight. Burn all your bridges. Go home and wake her and tell her tonight, "I'm going away and I'm never coming back".

WILL: Burn all my bridges! Yes.

VI: Yes.

WILL: Burn this one.

VI: If you like. I would. *[pause]* And only look ahead. Never look back.

WILL: Don't look back.

VI: And you won't be afraid.

WILL: And it won't even hurt.

VI: You said it yourself — from here go to Africa, Norway, anywhere. Look forward.

WILL: Or even Nova Scotia.

VI: Yes. *[she leans over the barrier]* Nova Scotia.

WILL: We'll go straight down to Marlow, through Oxford, then Gloucestershire, out to the sea, past South Wales....

VI: We'll keep moving....

WILL: Straight under Ireland and into the ocean....

VI: And we'll never look back....

WILL: And we won't be afraid.

VI: I'm not afraid, I'm not afraid....

WILL: I can't hear you.

VI: *[shouts louder]* I'm not afraid, I'm not afraid, I'm not afraid, I'm not afraid.

    [Vi leans dangerously far out and spreads her arms like wings. Will grabs her legs to steady her. She laughs.]

WILL: Vi, what are you...?

VI: I'm flying, look. I'm flying. I'm up high.

WILL: What d' you see?

VI: I'm lit up. My face is all lit up. Over the sea. Over the mountains. Lights, I see lights. They're fish. Luminous fish. And I follow the needles spinning in the glass — there are boats, little boats, but they're not boats, they're stars. There are stars in the sea, there are fish in the sky. I can read what they say, they say North, they say West, they say shshshshshshshsh, shshshshsh. They say safe. They say sure. But there's more, now, it's changing, there are forests with trees, there are mountains with pine — you can smell them, you can feel them, I can reach with my hands, there are birds, but they're tiny. I might break them, I could touch but they're tiny. I might... I might... it's gone dark, and I'm falling, going under, won't go under, going down, no control, no... no... no....

    [Will pulls her back from the barrier and holds her.]

WILL: It's alright.

VI: No control.

WILL: Yes, I know.

VI: Not afraid.

WILL: Vi, I'm here.

VI: Don't look back.

WILL: Vi, you're safe. *[he hugs her]* You're alright.

          [She pushes him away and breathes.]

VI: I was flying.

WILL: Yes.

          [Vi laughs.]

VI: I'm exhausted.

WILL: I know.

VI: Was it...?

WILL: What?

VI: Was it good?

WILL: It was lovely. It was lovely.

          [They laugh.]

SCENE SEVEN

[Drawing room of the Couth's house. Therese sits at her embroidery frame. The work is almost finished. Su is taking notes. She reads aloud from a small notebook.]

SU: Right, so clockwise, starting with yourself, it's Fanshaw, Carlyle, Wilkinson, Waldegrave, Fotheringay, Mr William, Fanshawe, Pilkington, Bathurst, Clayton, Fotheringay.

THERESE: Now. Procedure.

SU: Soup spoons, fish knives and forks, dessert spoons and forks, cheese knives and forks. Sherry glass, white wine glass, red wine glass, water tumbler. After the savoury, clear the table of everything but the candles.

          [Will enters. Su pauses. He motions to her to continue.]

          Bring fruit plates, finger bowls and fruit knives and forks. After the fruit bring amaretti, sugared almonds, marron glaces. After the sweetmeats, the port and the brandy.

THERESE: Have you checked the cellar book?

WILL: I thought I'd do it later.

THERESE: Have you ever decanted port, Susan?

SU: No, mum.

THERESE: Ask cook.

WILL: I can do it myself.

THERESE: There's no need.

WILL: I'll enjoy it.

THERESE: As you wish.

SU: Vi could do it.

WILL: I'll ask her. Where is she?

SU: Cleaning the step.

THERESE: That is not Violet's job.

SU: She offered to do it.

THERESE: That is not the point.

SU: She likes it outside.

WILL: I don't see it matters who cleans the step so long as the step is cleaned.

[Pause.]

THERESE: That will be all.

SU: Mum.

[Su leaves.]

WILL: I'm sorry but it's true.

THERESE: Is it?

WILL: You know it is.

THERESE: Do I?

WILL: Yes.

THERESE: Suddenly you are a mind-reader. You should buy a monkey and join the circus.

WILL: The party can be cancelled.

THERESE: This house is my business. The efficient running of it is all that is left to me. You are only passing through. Kindly remember that. There is a great deal to prepare. It is the last thing I shall do for you, and I shall do it as well as I am able.

WILL: I don't want to leave with bad feeling between us.

THERESE: Then don't.

WILL: I must.

THERESE: You don't understand. I'm old.

WILL: You're not old. You've been ill.

THERESE: I have seen the things old people see. I am old. Suddenly. Overnight. And I am not ready. And now soon I will die.

WILL: You are not going to die. If I thought for a minute you were going to die I would stay here.

THERESE: If I died you would stay. But because I am alive, you are going.

WILL: There isn't the time for this.

THERESE: Your time moves more quickly than mine. I shall have days like years to remember this. But you... you will control time. Change the future, change the past. And when you are closer to Canada than England this conversation will never have taken place. But I will have years of hearing it echo around this room. Years and years. Even if I die tomorrow.

[Pause.]

WILL: Listen to me. I cannot say this again. I love you. You know that. I love you. But I cannot change the fact that you are alone. It is not my place. It is not within my power.

THERESE: Not just alone. *[pause]* It is the dark also.

WILL: What is?

THERESE: By myself, in the dark. And no one heard. I spoke, but no one heard.

WILL: When did you?

THERESE: And I didn't recognise my own voice. I had no feeling, but a pain, and a voice I didn't recognise. And then I was the pain. And the pain was all that was left. And I didn't know my voice because it was the voice of someone completely and forever alone. And I didn't think I could be such a person. Not until then.

WILL: *[understanding her]* The stroke.

THERESE: And I am getting better, now.

WILL: Yes.

THERESE: But I cannot see the point.

             [Silence.]

WILL: How am I supposed to leave you?

THERESE: How are you supposed to stay?

             [There is a pause and then Therese starts sewing.]

WILL: There's a lot of work in this.

THERESE: Just one stitch after the next.

             [Will takes a deep breath.]

WILL: Ask me to stay and I will.

             [Therese savours the moment, then:]

THERESE: If I am to finish in time, you will have to step out of my light.

[Will leaves. Therese sews on.]

SCENE EIGHT

[The Couth's pantry. Vi runs in, pulling on her father's overcoat. Su chases after her, wearing a starched apron and cap and carrying Vi's.]

SU: Vi! Wait! Go back and apologise! It's not too late.

VI: Apologise?

SU: You didn't say anything up there, did you?

VI: What could I say?

SU: We'll tell 'em you were sick, that's why you ran out.

[Su tries to force Vi's uniform back on her.]

VI: I didn't run, I walked. I just walked.

SU: Okay. Only come on now.

VI: No! I'm not going back.

SU: But what happened?

VI: Something awful. Awful, d'you understand?

SU: Vi, tell me. Let me help you.

VI: He smiled at me. Do you see?

SU: Smiled?

VI: He smiled at me. Up there. In front of all those people. His people. Right in my face. Like a torch shining in my face. As if it was alright to do that. With me in my — this *[points to uniform]* — and him... him all...

SU: Vi?

VI: I've been so stupid.

SU: No...

VI: But not any more. I've got to go now.

SU: No, Vi. Please don't. I'll serve the dessert, I don't mind....

VI: I've got to go.

SU: Cook says I've to pack up your things. Leave 'em out the back. Not to let you back in.

VI: My things?

SU: Now d'you see?

   [Vi thinks hard, she panics, her mind races.]

VI: I can't. I musn't be late. I've got to keep my word. Even though he won't.

SU: Who?

VI: He'll still be up there.

SU: Who?

VI: Drinking his port and smiling.

   [Su is shocked.]

SU: Him?

VI: Not like you think.

SU: All along?

VI: No.

SU: I can't help you any more, Vi.

VI: It's not what you think, Su.

SU: I'd like to, but....

VI: Su?

SU: I'd like to show I was your friend, but I don't see there's any way now.

VI: No.

SU: I'll have to get back or it'll be me next.

VI: Yes.

SU: I'll put your things outside, but I'll leave the window open.

VI: Thanks.

SU: But I'll see you again sometime.

VI: I don't know.

SU: I think I shall.

[Su slips away. Vi calls after her.]

VI: Susie Owen! If I could have a friend, I think it would be you.

SCENE NINE

[The Couth's Kitchen. Will sits at the table, his head resting on the embroidered pillowslip on the tabletop. His packed bags and trunk are in the room. Vi sidles in, watches him for a while, then says:]

VI: You didn't come.

WILL: No.

VI: I waited anyway.

WILL: Sorry.

VI: I was glad in the end.

WILL: I got caught up.

VI: I think I'm better than you are.

WILL: I think that's probably right.

VI: Can't sleep then?

WILL: No.

VI: Shame.

WILL: I'm deserting my mother, my sick mother, just as my father did before me — an act which I despised — and now I'm going to Nova Scotia to learn to be more like him.

VI: Don't go then.

WILL: I've got to go. I have to take your button.

[He shows her the button round his neck.]

VI: Don't do anything on my account.

WILL: And you have my magnet.

VI: Yes. *[Vi considers the exchange]*

WILL: I think you'll make a great navigator one day, Violet.

VI: I hope so.

WILL: Better than me. You're not afraid of where you're going.

VI: No. I'm looking forward to it.

WILL: Eyes fixed on the horizon.

VI: That's right.

WILL: And me? I don't know how to leave.

VI: You don't know much if you don't know that.

WILL: My great escape.

VI: Why tell me this? Why do you think you can tell me all this? Because I'm paid to listen, is that it? I saw you up there. At your party. Just like yourself you were. As if it's enough to be that way.

WILL: How did you want me to be?

VI: Different.

WILL: Why?

VI: Because I was. Because I had no choice. Because

58

it's not enough for me to be who I am. And you have no right to look at me. Not up there. You have no right. You disgust me.

WILL: I never meant to upset you.

VI: What did you think you were doing with me all this time?

WILL: I don't know. I didn't think.

VI: What did you want from me?

WILL: I thought you'd be my salvation.

VI: Your what?

WILL: Show me how to get away.

VI: Why would I want to do that?

WILL: Not want to. By example.

VI: Example?

WILL: Your face. All lit up.

VI: Oh. Burning bridges, you mean.

WILL: Will you show me?

VI: I don't know. There's something going very fast I can't keep up with. In my head. And in my skin. Very fast, but I can't make it out.

[He kisses her on the cheek.]

WILL: Will you show me?

VI: Who are you now?

WILL: Who are you?

VI: Not myself. *[he kisses her on the neck]* If I help you, what will it mean?

WILL: Whatever you want.

VI: Nothing. I want it to mean nothing. As if it never happened. It's only because things need an ending.

I want it to be in the past.

[Will slips her father's coat from her shoulders and hangs it over a chair.]

WILL: This isn't what I thought, you know.

VI: That's because you don't think hard enough.

[Will puts his pillow on the floor. He picks up Vi and lays her on her back, hips resting on the pillow. He sits astride her.]

WILL: How's that?

VI: Alright.

WILL: Are you sure?

VI: It's alright. *[he starts to rub against her]* When will you leave?

WILL: The cab gets here at five.

VI: It'll just be getting light.

WILL: I wish I was taking you with me.

VI: I wouldn't want that.

WILL: Remember.

[He shows her the button.]

VI: I thought that would be something, but now I'm not sure. The stone's cold on my back.

[Will rolls away from her and pulls her on top of him, lifting her skirt.]

WILL: Here. You sit here.

VI: Maybe it's just a button after all.

[Will fumbles incompetently under her skirt.]

WILL: I'll never forget you, Vi. You know that, don't you? You'll always be special. I'll always remember the night on the bridge.

[Vi is distracted and cries out slightly when he starts to fuck her.]

The night on the bridge, Vi. That lovely, lovely night. A lovely night, Vi.

VI: What if this button is only a button? What knowledge of Nova Scotia then from this? I have a button missing from my shirt. You have a magnet missing from your pocket. What does that mean? Where does that leave us?

WILL: The night on the bridge, Vi....

VI: How d'you find things out then?

WILL: ...that night on the bridge...

VI: How're you supposed to find things out?

WILL: on the bridge... on the bridge... on the bridge...

VI: I want my button back.

[Will comes and pulls himself up to push his face into Vi's chest. She pushes him back down, hard. His head hits the stone floor.]

Will you listen to me?

[Will rubs his head. There is blood.]

WILL: Oh.

[He tries to lift himself onto his elbows, feels dizzy and lies down. Vi gets off him and wipes herself on her skirt. He is obviously in pain. Eventually, she places the pillow under his head.]

VI: Here.

WILL: You'd better get someone.

VI: In a minute.

WILL: I think I need a doctor.

VI: You'll be alright.

WILL: Get someone now.

VI: I can't. I've had the sack.

WILL: Go and get someone.

VI: It's only a bump.

WILL: It feels strange.

VI: Well, it's bound to.

[Pause.]

WILL: Vi?

[He reaches out his hand. She takes it.]

VI: *[without commitment]* Sh. I'm here now. Can you lift up your head?

[She lifts his head and starts to pull the button from him.]

WILL: No. Get away.

VI: I want my button back.

WILL: It hurts, keep away. Get a doctor. For God's sake, get a doctor.

[Vi backs off him. He goes quiet and seems to drift into sleep. Vi is fretful, tries to occupy herself for a minute, wipes herself on her skirt, looks at the packed bags. She wants her button back. Vi then nudges Will, who does not respond. She shoves him, and there is still no response. She snatches the button thread and snaps it hard, pulling it from round his neck. Will suddenly takes a deep breath which he exhales as a long groan. He is absolutely still. Vi takes a closer look and puts her ear to his chest. Su enters, carrying a suitcase. She stops in her track when she sees Will. Vi shrugs.]

SU: What happened?

VI: I don't know.

SU: What happened! *[Vi puts her ear to his face, to his chest.]* Come away, Vi.

VI: He just hit his head. On the back.

[She lifts his head. Su sees the blood.]

SU: Come away. *[Vi lets the head fall. Su pulls Vi to a chair and sits her down. She then checks the body, takes off her apron and covers his face]* You're in trouble, Vi.

VI: I think I must be.

SU: We have to get you away.

VI: I think I killed him.

SU: It was an accident.

VI: I pushed him.

SU: Pushed him off you. Any girl would do the same.

VI: You don't understand.

SU: Is there somewhere you can go, Vi?

VI: Not home.

SU: No, Vi. That's the first place they'll look.

VI: Will they come looking then?

SU: I think so.

VI: It was an accident.

SU: Anywhere else, Vi.

VI: No. He didn't make me, Su. I wanted to. But then he wouldn't listen so I pushed him, and then blood.

SU: What about the man in the letter. Your letter, Vi. Would he help?

[Vi pulls the letter out of her vest and gives it to Su.]

VI: My uncle. I could go there. Read this to me, Su.

SU: "Dear Violet... sorry to be the one to tell you, but your mam's been bad. She... she... she tried to finish herself last week with your da's razor, but our Kitty found her in time. She's staying with us now till she's better. Please send money if you can." I'm sorry, Vi.

[Vi takes back the letter and pores over the writing.]

VI: "Kitty". How could I be so wrong?

SU: We've got to get rid of him, Vi.

VI: Wrong by miles.

SU: We could say he was drunk when the cabbie came. Send him anyway. Cabbie could carry him. There must be somewhere you can go, Vi. Somewhere safe. Far away, where they won't look. Think of a place, Vi.

VI: Nova Scotia.

SU: What?

VI: That's where he was going. Nova Scotia.

SU: You could take him with you. In the trunk.

VI: No-va Sco-tia...

[Su goes through Will's pockets. Finds a wallet, passports, papers.]

SU: Get your clothes off, Vi. Come on. All of them. Now! *[Su opens the trunk and pulls out clothes]* You'll have to wear these. You'll be alright, Vi. Just like when you go out at night. You can do it, Vi. I know you can. And we'll have to cut your hair. Come on.

VI: Cut my hair?

SU: Get the sewing scissors.

VI: Cut my hair?

SU: Just get them, Vi. You've not got long. *[Su empties out the last of the trunk onto a pile]* Chuck your stuff on there. I'll burn it. *[Vi stands watching. Su pulls Vi's shirt off over her head]* Will you come on now?

[Vi pulls off her shirt, her shoes and her skirt. Su pushes one of Will's shirts on over her head and shoves a pair of trousers into her hands. Vi takes over dressing herself as Su lifts Will's head from the pillow and measures him against the trunk.]

He'll fit. Now. *[Su tries to lift Will but he's too heavy]* You're gonna have t'help me, Vi.

[Vi is appalled. Reluctantly she goes over and takes one end of the body. They drag it over and push it into the trunk. Su slams the lid shut.]

There. Okay. Where's the scissors?

[Vi looks blank. Su rushes to get them.]

VI: Don't cut my hair off, Su.

SU: I'm sorry.

VI: I don't want my hair cut off. It's all I've got left of me.

[Su handles the hair, scissors at the ready.]

SU: You've got lovely hair, Vi, but it's all the fashion now to wear it short. And I'll keep it for you, till you get back, I promise.

[A bell rings.]

VI: Cabbie!

[They look at the mess. Su stuffs the scissors in her pocket.]

SU: You just get your coat on ready.

[Su finds a bucket and scrubbing brush and scrubs hard at the bloodstain on the floor.]

65

Come on, get your coat!

[Vi pulls on her father's coat. Su talks as she scrubs, not looking at Vi.]

You can do it, Vi. I know you can.

[Vi feels the weight of the coat on her and takes comfort from it.]

SU: There!

[Su throws the brush back into the bucket and sees Vi.]

Oh. No, Vi. Wait here.

[Su goes and returns with a navy cashmere top coat on a hanger. The bell rings again. Su holds up the coat.]

I'm sorry, Vi.

VI: No? Like new it is.

SU: I know.

VI: Good as new.

SU: Come on, now.

[Vi peels off her father's coat. Su helps her on with Will's. As Vi feels the weight of Will's coat she seems to grow to fill it. Su turns back the long sleeves and stands back to admire Vi.]

You better get going.

VI: Will you do something for me, Susie? Say my name. Say my name to me.

[Pause.]

SU: Vi. Violet Evans.

VI: My name is Violet Evans, and I am not afraid.

[Vi and Su kiss, very gently on the lips. The bell rings again and they part. Vi reaches into her father's pocket, takes out the magnet and gives it to Su.]

SU: What is it?

VI: It's for you, Susie.

SU: It's a magnet.

VI: It's a prayer.

[Su puts the magnet in her pocket. With one hand she gently takes hold of Vi's hair at the back of her neck. The other hand steals slowly to the scissors. In a single movement, the hair falls to the ground.]

[Blackout. End of Act One.]

Act Two

SCENE ONE

[New Waterford, Nova Scotia. Vi's room in a smart boarding house. Vi stands in her shirt sleeves — a long shirt whose tails hang out over the men's trousers she wears. There is a waistcoat and jacket on a hanger. She runs her fingers over them, turning the hanger with the pressure. Will enters and stands behind her. He assumes a dancing position, his arms held out, as if waiting for a partner. He wears the clothes he died in. He has a bloody patch on the back of his head.]

VI: Not now. I don't want to do that now.

WILL: Sooner or later you've got to.

VI: I said not now.

    [She turns to face him. She is sleepy, just woken from a nightmare. Her heart beats very fast.]

    This can be undone. I didn't do this. Who did this? Who did this?

WILL: Violet....

VI: Don't say that name! Don't you ever say that name.

WILL: It's all or nothing.

VI: Yes. There's no going back. I understand that. We have to go on. It's just... I had a bad dream. Or is this the bad dream?

    [He resumes the position, bored.]

    Not that. Not yet.

WILL: You want them to find out?

VI: No.

WILL: You want to be safe?

VI: Yes.

WILL: Then you have to learn to dance.

VI: Yes. Yes, I do.

[Will holds out his arms. She tries to summon the courage to embrace him. Eventually she approaches, puts her arms around him, gags and pulls away. Vi fights not to be sick.]

WILL: Not again.

VI: We'll do it later.

WILL: You ought to get it over with.

VI: I said later. I am in charge here. We do as I say.

WILL: I see.

[Vi offers her hand to Will.]

VI: Pinch me. *[He does. She cries out]* I'll get dressed then.

[Will takes the waistcoat and jacket off the hanger. Vi slips them on, spruces herself up, tucks herself in, and waits for Will's approval.]

WILL: Not bad. You should be fat enough to leave the last two buttons of the waistcoat open.

VI: You're not.

WILL: It was my father's.

VI: You never told me that.

WILL: You didn't ask. Undo the buttons. *[she does]* Puff yourself up a bit. *[she tries]* You've got to fill the suit. *[Vi rearranges herself in the suit and grows]* Good. You've been getting sloppy. You need to concentrate.

VI: I do.

WILL: It would only take one of these boys to notice.

VI: They won't.

WILL: That cabin boy noticed.

VI: Weeks ago. I've improved since then. Anyway, what was he going to say about it?

WILL: These boys will be different.

VI: They need work, don't they? So. They wouldn't care if I was a dog.

WILL: *Were* a dog.

VI: Were. They wouldn't care if I were a dog. How long've they been waiting?

WILL: The first one's been here all night. There are thirty or so behind him already.

VI: He'll be tired then.

WILL: Yes.

VI: He'll never notice.

WILL: You ought to see them all. It's good practice.

VI: I know when I've found the one.

WILL: Don't wave your arms about so.

[He stuffs one of his hands into a trouser pocket. Vi mimics him.] Better. Now....

[He waves his arm for her to walk up and down the room. She does so. It's quite good. Will locks his hands behind his back. She copies him. He emphasises the pull back of his shoulders. She copies him and paces again — increasingly convincing. Will slaps his thighs, spreads his feet slightly further apart, toes pointing slightly outwards. Vi adjusts the walk accordingly.]

Yes, It's getting there. It's much better.

[*There is a knock at the door. Will indicates the seat. Vi sits down.*]

Now remember, take your time. And fill the chair. [*she does*] Good. You'll be fine.

VI: Why're you helping me?

WILL: Because there's no one else who can.

[*There is another knock ut the door. Vi focuses, then says:*]

VI: Come!

[*Davie enters. He is very energised, potentially aggressive and nervous. Vi sifts through a pile of papers. Davie fights to keep his energy up.*]

DAVIE: Sir?

VI: Yes, yes. [*Vi messes with the papers a moment longer. Davie wilts*] Right. You are?

DAVIE: Davie Maclean, sir. About the advertisement.

VI: You've worked as a chauffeur before?

DAVIE: Yes, sir. I was with Ford Bloxley for nearly a year.

VI: Ford who?

DAVIE: Ford Bloxley. He used to run the power plant.

VI: Reason for leaving?

DAVIE: Mr Bloxley went home. Back to Illinois.

VI: And when was that?

DAVIE: Seven, eight months back.

VI: And since then?

DAVIE: Well... some labouring... but I should tell you Mr Bloxley was a big man around here and....

VI: Casual work?

71

DAVIE: Yes, but I have a reference from Mr Bloxley here....

VI: But since then only casual work?

DAVIE: Yes.

VI: All here in New Waterford.

DAVIE: Now look, I'm a hard worker, Mr Couth, and I'll turn my hand to anything but... there's nothing...

VI: The reference. *[Davie offers it and tries to calm himself.]* Just read it out to me, could you. You can read?

DAVIE: Yes, I can read.

VI: I'll trust you to be honest.

DAVIE: I am honest.

VI: The reference please....

DAVIE: "Davie Maclean has been in my employ for six months. In that time he has shown himself to be honest, sensible, clean and hardworking. He is a reliable driver and a first class handyman. Responsibility sits easily on his young shoulders. I do not hesitate to recommend his services." And it's signed by him, here, look.

            [He shows Vi.]

VI: Very nice.

DAVIE: Yes.

VI: Good. This Bloxley character, why did he leave?

DAVIE: I think he wasn't making money any more.

VI: I see.

DAVIE: A man like that needs a lot of money.

VI: I'm sure. There are a lot of other boys who want this job.

DAVIE: I know that, sir.

VI: Need this job, you might say.

DAVIE: Yes, sir.

VI: Why should I take you and not one of them?

         [For a moment, Davie is baffled.]

DAVIE: I can't answer that, sir.

VI: No?

DAVIE: That's for you to decide.

VI: You live at home, with your family?

DAVIE: Yes, sir.

VI: And your father is in work?

DAVIE: Mr Couth, my father is a miner.

VI: And is he among the men striking?

DAVIE: He is, sir.

VI: What do you think I've come all this way for?

DAVIE: To break the strike, I guess.

VI: And does your father know you've applied here?

DAVIE: He does, sir.

VI: And does he approve?

DAVIE: No, sir, he does not.

VI: Money must be tight at home.

DAVIE: A little.

VI: How are you living?

DAVIE: No worse than anyone else.

VI: But without money?

DAVIE: We get credit at Company Stores....

VI: Really? But this job would make a difference.

DAVIE: Yes.

VI: If I gave you this job, I'd expect you to work hard.

DAVIE: That's what I want. More than the money, even. A chance to work. I need to work.

VI: And I would also need to be assured of your... discretion. I couldn't have information leaking out from my office.... You might find yourself in a rather awkward position.

DAVIE: You need a driver and I can drive. I need a job and you can give me one. I'm not a liar or a spy. When you wanted me I'd be right there, and when you didn't it'd be as if I didn't exist. I won't give you any trouble. I'll be worthy of your confidence, Mr Couth. Those are simple facts, sir....

VI: Tell me....

DAVIE: ...Davie.

VI: ...Davie. If I were to offer you the position, when could you start?

DAVIE: If you offered me the position? Well... now. Whenever you want.

VI: Tomorrow will be fine. Corporation dinner and dance. I'm addressing the Board beforehand, so I'll need you here by six.

DAVIE: Six.

VI: Sharp.

DAVIE: I've got the job.

VI: There'll be a two-week trial period.

DAVIE: A trial. Yes, sir. Thank you. You won't regret this.

VI: I hope not.

DAVIE: Six. Sharp. *[Vi indicates the door. Davie backs out, tripping over himself]* Sir. *[he is gone]*

[Vi exhales a huge sigh — relief and excitement. She is very pleased with herself.]

WILL: Good.

VI: Very good! I... I enjoyed it.

WILL: I could see that.

VI: You see! He never suspected. Too many other worries.

WILL: The trial period was an inspiration.

VI: He'll be so scared for that two weeks it'll never enter his head, and after that he'll be so used to me he won't notice. He was desperate. I could feel it. And weak. Honest and over-emotional, over-developed sense of loyalty. He's perfect.

WILL: It is uncanny.

VI: Quite the little gentleman, aren't I?

WILL: Something like that.

VI;   And if we can pull off this dinner, we'll be made.

WILL: You need more practice.

VI: I'm hardly going to pick up the wrong fork, am I? I've set them often enough.

WILL: What about the dancing?

VI: No. I'd never fool a woman. I'll sit them all out.

WILL: People will talk. It might be taken as a slight.

VI: Bad leg, old boy. Nasty fall playing polo. Hey ho.

          [Will is impressed/appalled.]

WILL: Oh yes, it's very good.

VI: And that boy's given me some ideas for the speech.

WILL: It's frighteningly good.

VI: We'll have to go in hard. It's the only way I'm safe.

75

WILL: And you must be safe.

VI: Yes. Yes, I must.

SCENE TWO

[The Couth's drawing room, dimly lit. Therese sits in a bath chair, staring ahead. Su enters carrying a tray. She sets it down on the table next to Therese.]

SU: Awake then? Yes. I thought you might be havin' a bit of a nap, you know. To keep your strength up.

[Su rearranges the cushions behind Therese]

I've brought your milk and liver. And that's not all, mum. I've got you a bit of a treat today.

[She spreads a napkin in Therese's lap.]

But it's for afters. Here you go then.

[She proffers a glass of thick, pinky brown liquid. Therese closes her eyes.]

You really should have a sip.

[Nothing. Su puts the glass down on the tray.]

In a minute then. Shall I tell you the treat?

[Su takes a bag of sweets out of her pocket. Shows Therese.]

Barley sugars. For when you've finished the liver. To take away the taste. I'll put them on the tray where you can see them.

[Su looks out of the window.]

It's nice out. Chilly, but bright enough. I'd like to get shot of these shades. Still. Not till you're better doctor says. P'raps it'll give you somethin' to look forward to. They say it might snow if it warms up a bit. But I don't see it. Sky's too clear if you ask me. *[pause]* Shall we have another go at lunch?

[Su lifts the glass to Therese's face. Therese turns her head away very slightly. Su puts down the glass and tries to control her anger.]

I could make you. You know that, don't you? No one would blame me. I'd say well she's not touched a thing for a fortnight. I had to do something. I'd be in trouble enough if you did starve. Anyone else'd force it down you. What could you do? I mean think about it. Absolutely nothing. Anyone else'd hold your nose and tip it down you, and let it go all over your chin and dribble down your front. Anyone else would feed you like a baby, Mrs Couth. They'd tuck your napkin in your neck and they'd make you eat. *[pause]* But I won't. And don't ask me why not. I just won't. Let's do some exercises.

[Su takes a sock ball out of her apron pocket. She places it in Therese's hand and curls the fingers round it.]

Here we go. Now squeeze.

[Therese doesn't move. Su takes the hand and opens and closes the fingers round the soft ball.]

One, and two, and three, and four, and five, and six, and seven, and eight. Very good. Other hand. One, and two, and three, and four, and five, and six, and seven, and eight. That's that then. Now. Can you try and point your toes for me?

[Nothing.]

Good. No. Okay then.

[Su kneels on the floor and flexes Therese's foot, counting as before. Repeat with the other foot.]

Good. Very good. Incredible progress. How long are we supposed to go on like this then, eh? You and me? How long? You can't just wish yourself to death. It isn't fair. I know you're on your own now, but so am I. And if you were meant to be gone you would be by now. You've just got to have faith, that something will happen. That you'll make something happen. So have faith, Mrs Couth, if you can. And I'll get rid of this muck.

[Su puts a piece of barley sugar on the table and takes the tray.]

I'll leave you this in case you fancy it later. You know where I am.

[Su leaves. Therese looks at the barley sugar. She closes her eyes against tears. Lights dim to a murky winter dusk.]

SCENE THREE

[The Dominion Coal and Power Corporation Dinner and Dance. There is a general hubbub, the sound of voices — all male. The gentlemen of the board are gathered together. Vi takes up her place at the head of the table. She stands with her hands on it, leaning slightly forward, braced. She rings a small bell set on the table before her. The talking subsides. Will appears beside her.]

WILL: Take your time, remember.

[Vi faces out the board until there is complete silence. She holds her focus for a second, then begins.]

VI: Gentlemen of the board. Can I say, first of all....

WILL: May I, not can I. We know you are able the question is one of permission.

[Vi is thrown for a second, regains her composure, continues:]

VI: May I say, right away, what a pleasure it is to be here tonight...

WILL: "This evening" is better.

VI: ... to be here this evening...

WILL: Relax. You're trying too hard. Don't forget gestures.

VI: ...to be here this evening...

WILL: The gestures. Come on now. *[Vi gazes out, afraid, into the crowd.]* There's no going back.

           [Vi collects herself, draws herself up, starts to come alive as "Will".]

VI: ...to be here this evening... in spite of the difficult circumstances that bring us together.

           [Her gestures now are choreographed, mirrored by Will who stands slightly behind her. They are absolutely precise with his — when she shifts her weight, turns her head, fingers her jacket, etc.]

           The first rule of war, gentlemen — and that is more or less the situation we are facing here — is "know thine enemy". I believe that in this area I may be of considerable use.

           I know our enemy. Their fears, desires, strengths and weaknesses. I know their habits and what remains of their resources. And this leads me to say something which some of you may find shocking: the longer the strike goes on the better.

           [Will misses a beat. When she resumes, he struggles to catch up.]

           Yes. The longer they keep this up the further they play into our hands. They exhaust themselves without you or I having to lift a finger and then they will accept whatever terms we choose to impose. But I would propose that we hasten the inevitable end, and as an immediate action, cut off credit at Company Stores.

           [A ripple of surprise and objections. Will is appalled. He stops mirroring her. Vi talks down the objections.]

Gentlemen. I do appreciate that this is a harsh response, but the situation worsens day by day because no one saw fit to take action sooner. Then it might have been possible to deal tactically, nip rebellion in the bud. But it is too late for that now. I stand here before you in my father's stead. It falls to me to defend his investment, and defend it I must. As a matter of duty. Of honour. This must be the last strike. Let us grind the enemy under heel so it can never ever threaten us again. We must be absolutely certain that we are safe.

We have a responsibility to the past to impose order here. Our enemy is determined to return this place to chaos and wilderness. That cannot be permitted. So join me gentlemen: cut off credit, break this strike, and let's all have a future to look forward to.

[Vi beats the table with her fist. There is a roar of support and applause, which fades to Will's slow clapping. Vi is ecstatic.]

It was easy.

[Will continues clapping.]

They loved it.

[He continues.]

Stop that.

[He doesn't.]

Stop it!

[She stops his hands. He grabs her. She squeals, pulls away, but he holds fast and speaks into her face.]

Get off!

WILL: A future to look forward to, is that it?

VI: Let me go.

80

WILL: And what about the past?

           [She pushes him off her with a great shove.]

VI;   No! I've found a place where no one knows me. I can be who I want.

WILL: And this is who you want to be?

VI: He'll do. For now.

WILL: Starving them out.

VI: Yes.

WILL: You've seen all this before, haven't you?

VI: I'll give them a month without credit.

WILL: You might be wrong, though. It might not work.

VI: They still have power down there. While there's power there's water. I'll cut it in a month if nothing's changed.

WILL: Just like that?

VI: I will do what is necessary. Whatever is necessary.

SCENE FOUR

[The Couth's drawing room. Su comes in carrying a tray.]

SU: (Awake then? Yes. I thought you might've been havin' a little nap, you know. To keep your strength up.) You haven't touched your barley sugar, look. Oh well. I don't suppose you're going to drink this either, are you? I'll have to be honest with you, Mrs Couth. If this goes on for another week you're gong to die, and I'll be off elsewhere. Now in some ways, Mrs Couth, that would suit me right down to the ground. I could go somewhere friendly. A big place with a bit of company. A family with daughters. Dressing up and parties.

That sort of thing. But you're not the only one waiting. And if I leave here, how will I be found? So you've got to live. Because waiting is an important job, and someone's got to do it. And it just so happens that it's got to be me and you.

[Su picks up the untouched tray.]

I know you can hear me, Mrs Couth. I'm sorry, but I won't just let you go. I need you to live, and that's all there is to it. I can't just let you go. So you better buck up your ideas. Tomorrow is another day. And that's a threat as well as a promise.

[Su takes away the tray and leaves.]

SCENE FIVE

[Vi's room. Vi and Davie enter. There is flour all over their clothes and across Vi's face. She wipes it away, furious.]

VI: Well how did they know where I live?

DAVIE: I don't know, sir.

[Vi tears off her jacket.]

VI: Did you recognise them?

DAVIE: Sir?

VI: I want their names.

DAVIE: I don't know, sir.

[Davie brushes away at Vi's jacket.]

VI: When I lived in a town like this I knew all the names. I knew all the faces.

DAVIE: It was dark, sir.

VI: They were after you too, remember.

DAVIE: I know, sir.

VI: Well then?

DAVIE: Really, sir.

VI: I want their names.

DAVIE: But I just don't know.

[Vi gives up, takes off her waistcoat, hurls it at Davie and shouts out of the door.]

VI: Bloody funny way to behave for people who reckon they've got no food, wouldn't you say? *[Davie shakes the waistcoat]* Well?

Davie: Yes, sir.

[Vi shouts out again.]

VI: Could've knocked up four good big tin loaves with that bag of flour! *[she paces and plans]* We'll need an extra lock on this door now.

DAVIE: Sir.

VI: They've made a big mistake this time. I'll tell you that. They've made a big mistake. I'll bring in a curfew. This won't happen again. They'll be sorry. Understand?

DAVIE: Yes, sir.

VI: I mean it.

DAVIE: I understand.

VI: Do you hear me?

DAVIE: I do, sir.

VI: I'd like a glass of water.

DAVIE: Yes, sir.

VI: And get rid of these. *[she points to the jacket and the waistcoat]*

DAVIE: I'll get them cleaned up. Really clean, sir.

83

VI: I don't want to see them again.

DAVIE: No, sir. Good. What should I...?

VI: I never want to see them again.

[Davie takes the jacket and goes out. Vi struggles to keep her grip. Without her overclothes we see that she is fatter than before. She sits in her chair and easily fills it. Will enters. Davie enters carrying a tray with a glass of water on it.]

DAVIE: Your water, sir.

[Vi sits, exhausted. She then goes to pick up the glass.]

VI: Water is served in a tumbler. This is a white wine glass.

DAVIE: A tumbler.

VI: Yes.

DAVIE: I'll change it right away, sir. *[he takes the tray]* I'm learning all the time, sir. In fact, sir, can I say something?

VI: "May I", Davie. We know you are able, the question is one of permission.

DAVIE: May I, sir?

VI: Please.

DAVIE: I wanted to thank you for finding me these extra chores here. It makes a big difference with things as they are. Not just the money side, but other things.

VI: Very good.

DAVIE: You see, it's different for you. You can follow in your father's footsteps.

VI: What?

DAVIE: Working here. But I can't do that. My father's footsteps don't lead anywhere, you see. Not now. I needed someone to follow. That's all. *[pause]* I'll get

84

	the water.
VI:	Yes.
DAVIE:	And then I'll do the shoes.
VI:	Right.
DAVIE:	I'll be polishing the soles like you said.

[Will enters. Davie goes to leave.]

| WILL: | Ancient history. |
| VI: | Oh shut up. |

[Davie turns back.]

DAVIE:	Sir?
VI:	I... I thought you spoke.
DAVIE:	No, sir.

[Davie leaves.]

WILL:	Careless.
VI:	Go away.
WILL:	And after you've been doing so well.
VI:	It won't work.
WILL:	What?
VI:	I'm safe now.
WILL:	Is that why you've got the army at the ready?
VI:	Merely a precaution.
WILL:	People will get hurt.
VI:	In case of public disturbance.
WILL:	Do you understand?
VI:	The police can't cope.
WILL:	Killed, even.

VI: I can't help that. They should just back down. *[Davie returns with a tumbler. Vi takes it and drinks]* Of course we're lucky to have fresh water up here. Is the power still out at your end of town?

WILL: What do you think?

DAVIE: They say it'll be fixed by the end of the week.

[Davie gets on with cleaning the shoes. Will watches him.]

VI: Isn't that what they said a fortnight ago?

DAVIE: You know there are people who think it's deliberate?

VI: You think someone would cut off the power and the water on purpose?

WILL: Surely not!

DAVIE: I told them no. I said I would have heard something. You would have said something. Warned me.

VI: Well of course.

WILL: Naturally.

DAVIE: I mean we all want this finished one way or another, but there're limits.

WILL: Hear that?

VI: Quite. Although it would be easier to help if they showed a little more sign of compliance.

DAVIE: That's what I told 'em.

VI: Are they making trouble for you?

[Davie considers this.]

WILL: Do you really need to ask?

DAVIE: Let's say I'm kind of an outsider now.

WILL: They think he betrays them.

VI: They think you betray them?

DAVIE: Maybe, but it's not true. I don't betray them.

VI: No. That's the spirit.

WILL: "That's the spirit." Very good. It's very good. Just look at you. So much more like myself than I could ever have been. It's almost as if I never died. But someone died, didn't they?

VI: How're the shoes coming?

DAVIE: I won't be a minute.

WILL: He's a good little worker.

VI: Very good.

WILL: And I must say he's making the most fantastic job of them.

VI: Very good. You're making a very good job of them.

DAVIE: Sir.

WILL: Not as good as you, of course. But then you were exceptional. *[Vi struggles to hold her temper]* Always the perfect servant. *[Will musn't win]* Hardly knew we had you. Like a ghost about the place. *[Vi cries out to silence Will]*

VI: That's enough. No pain! *[Davie drops the shoes. Vi fights to stay in control]* No pain, no gain, Davie. There's a thing I've been putting off. A thing I've got to get rid of, do you understand? *[Davie is silent. He nods. Vi is on terrifying form]* A thing that's been making me ill. And it'll have to go. It'll have to go right away. Today. Now.

WILL: D'you think this'll work?

VI: And when it's gone, things will all seem much clearer. It's a trunk I need to get rid of.

DAVIE: Trunk.

VI: Should've dumped it sooner — ages ago, but what with — you know — one thing and another — it's full, you see — it's full of food!

DAVIE: Food.

VI: Yes. So where could we get rid of it?

DAVIE: None of it could be salvaged?

WILL: Nasty!

VI: God no! Absolutely not. I want it gone. Completely.

DAVIE: There's dumping ground about a mile north of here. If you leave it to me I'll do it tomorrow.

VI: That's no good. I thought perhaps in the sea.

DAVIE: Might get caught in the slipstream, wash straight back in.

WILL: That wouldn't do.

VI: No, no. That musn't happen.

DAVIE: We'd have to do it at night to catch the tide.

VI: Fine.

DAVIE: Where is it now?

VI: In the cellar.

DAVIE: The cellar here?

VI: Yes.

DAVIE: Uh-oh. It's probably full of mice, maggots, god knows what. You okay?

WILL: No, she's not.

VI: I'm fine. It's just remembering the smell of it in the cabin on the way here.

DAVIE: You had it in your cabin?

VI: Yes.

DAVIE: Can I ask exactly what's in it?

VI: Yes. Pork.

DAVIE: Pork.

WILL: So you think I'll disappear once you're rid of the trunk?

DAVIE: We'll burn it. Take it up the cliff like you say, then burn it. Let the water have what's left.

VI: Fine.

WILL: And then you can pretend it never happened.

DAVIE: I'll take a look at it now. Check it'll fit in the car.

VI: Go ahead.

            [Davie leaves.]

WILL: Is that the idea?

VI: I don't know what you're talking about.

WILL: Then why am I here?

VI: Maybe you're not.

WILL: So why are you talking to me?

VI: Might be talking to myself.

WILL: First sign of going mad.

VI: No, I thought.... *[she checks the palms of her hands, then stops herself and wipes them]* Perhaps I made you up.

WILL: Why would you do that?

VI: Because I needed you.

WILL: Didn't think you needed anyone.

VI: I don't. Not now.

WILL: Maybe I'm a punishment.

VI: What for?

WILL: The thing you can't remember.

VI: No. I think I made you up.

WILL: So what's in the trunk?

VI: Pork.

WILL: You don't expect anyone to believe that.

VI: I expect people to believe every word I say. It's what they're paid for. Whether they think I'm telling the truth or not. I'm in charge here now.

WILL: But you don't believe it.

VI: Yes. Yes, I do. I believe it absolutely.

           [Davie returns, wearing his scarf as a mask.]

DAVIE: Oh boy, that really is a mess down there. It's leakin' out all over the place, this sticky stuff, and the cellar is just buzzing.

VI: No.

DAVIE: Y'can hardly hear yourself think f'the flies. *[Vi shrieks at the floor. Davie looks at his shoes. There are wet footsteps behind him.]* Oh god, I've trodden it up here. I'm so sorry.

           [Vi stands on her chair.]

VI: You stupid, stupid boy. Get a bloody mop and clean it up.

DAVIE: Yes, sir.

           [Davie goes out.]

VI: Now! Run and clean it up. Hurry.

WILL: But you said it was only pork.

           [Davie runs back in with a mop.]

VI: It is, it is, it is only... nothing. It's nothing. This is merely a precaution.

DAVIE: Sir?

VI: Just do as I tell you. Just do as you're bloody told.

           [Davie mops and mops at the floor. It is hard going. Physically, it recalls Su's cleaning of the blood at the end of Act One.].

           And don't let anything like this happen again.

DAVIE: No, sir.

VI: I want those marks gone.

DAVIE: I am really sorry, sir.

VI: I want them gone. I want it to look as though none of this ever happened. Understand?

DAVIE: Sir.

VI: I want it to be as good as new.

           [She stands terrified as Davie mops away. Will walks around the room, unseen by Davie, leaving more and more tracks. Davie mops for all he is worth. Chaos. Vi shouts to show Davie fresh tracks. He mops.]

           I want it all to be as good as new.

           [Vi puts her hands over her ears and closes her eyes.]

SCENE SIX

[The lights come up on Su, standing in a bright summer dress and cardigan, holding a bundle of drapes. Winter sun pours into the room. Su's eyes are closed. She feels the sun on her skin. Su takes out the drapes and returns with a tray. There is a small bowl on the tray and a hyacinth in a vase. She sets it down on Therese's side table. Su goes out again and returns wheeling Therese. She wheels her directly into the bright light. Therese can hardly bear it.]

SU: Yes. We're going to do things differently from now

91

on. From today, things will be different. You've got
to try. Now. Here's egg custard. Plenty of vanilla.
Very filling. You've got to eat it. Just a touch of
nutmeg. It'll do you good. You're never having
liver and milk again. I'll tell you that for nothing.
From now on, there's no doctor and we don't
pretend there's anyone who's going to come and
make things better. We just do it. Alright? I
brought you a hyacinth from the park, so you can
see Spring's not far away. I want you to smell it.
[Su smells it.] Mmm. It'll let you know you're still
alive. I'm off to fetch the tea. Yes. You're drinking
tea again. I've told you things had changed.

[Su goes out. Therese turns her head very slowly to look
at the flower. She hesitates, then leans towards it and
smells it. She breathes it in. She feels the sun on her
skin. Su returns with a pot of tea and two cups. She
pours out tea for two.]

I'm not wearing gloves any more either. If you say
I've got to then I 'spose I will, but they only make
me drop things all the time and I'm forever
washing 'em. My hands are clean as clean. Look.

[She shows Therese her hands. Therese looks at them.]

Here we go then.

[Su carefully lifts Therese's cup and saucer and places it
on her knee. She moves behind her and helps her to lift
the cup, holding the frail hands around the china.]

Steady, now. Steady.

[The cup reaches Therese's lips and she drinks a little.
Su gently lowers the cup back to the saucer.]

Thank you.

[She puts the cup and saucer back on the table.]

Alright?

[Very slowly, Therese nods.]

Yes, I thought so. I knew, in fact. Give me your hand. This one, nearest me.

[Therese looks down at her left hand. The thumb moves slightly.]

Good girl.

[Su lifts the hand and rubs it between her own.]

How's that then?

[Therese smiles.]

Can you feel that? Warmin' up a bit now, eh?

[Su rubs and rubs.]

Oh, it's lovely.

[Su puts the hand down gently. The fingers open and close a little.]

Let's try the other one.

[The other hand twitches. Su lift it up and rubs it.]

We'll get some life back into you if it's the last thing we do.

[She replaces the hand. The fingers flex a little.]

Now we're going to have some lunch, and then I'm going to read to you, and then we'll do more exercises. But we've got all day. So take your time.

[Su spreads the napkin in Therese's lap and takes a spoonful of the custard. She helps Therese's fingers round the spoon and lifts it to her mouth. Therese eats.]

Yes. That's what I thought. Exactly. That's exactly it. Yes.

SCENE SEVEN

[The clifftop. A fire crackles. A bell rings erratically in the distance. Vi looks down over the edge. Davie arrives.]

DAVIE: Don't get too close. It draws you down.

VI: It's rough.

DAVIE: Always is. Sir — I'm sorry about earlier. With the trunk.

VI: What's the bell?

DAVIE: Warning ships off the coast. *[pause]* What do you think will happen, Mr Couth?

VI: Happen how?

DAVIE: People're getting ill with the bad water. My sister's sick, in fact. People're scared. Angry.

VI: I'm sorry to hear that.

DAVIE: If something doesn't change soon there's gonna be trouble. There's a rally at the power plant tonight. It wouldn't take much to... I don't know, push things over the edge.

VI: That would be a shame.

DAVIE: Some people say the army'd come in. Troops've been moved nearby. They really believe it. That isn't true though, is it?

VI: What's wrong with your sister?

DAVIE: We're not sure.

VI: What does the doctor say?

DAVIE: She hasn't seen one.

VI: Well she should.

DAVIE: I know that.

VI: Oh.

           [Pause.]

DAVIE: I have a friend with a boat near here. When we were kids we used to pretend we were gonna row up to Greenland or over to England. Maybe go to

94

	Scotland, meet all my ancestors. Maclean, y'see. It's a Scottish name. I plan to leave some day, though.

VI: Your great escape.

DAVIE: I need to work. I mean really work. Not just to survive, but to know where I am. To have some pride, you know? To have a life I can feel around me. Something real. Maybe I'll go to England. They've work there, don't they?

VI: There're mining towns like New Waterford if that's what you're looking for.

DAVIE: I don't have the concentration for that. The last explosion here killed sixty-five and you still have to brush the gas out of the cracks with your coat down there. I couldn't do pit work.

VI: An explosion?

DAVIE: Last year. You musta heard about it?

VI: I lived in a place once where something like that happened.

DAVIE: Bad?

VI: Yes. Nearly 400 dead. *[Davie whistles. Vi is starting to remember]* And there was a man there who knew about it. He was a miner.

DAVIE: Knew about it?

VI: He had a special way of doing things, of preparing before the shift...

DAVIE: A routine.

VI: Exactly. But this day something went wrong. Something with a match, perhaps... I can't quite... but anyway, he knew he mustn't go today. And a few hours later, it went up. And afterwards he could never go back down. And his daughter — his little girl — she was the only girl on the street who still... still had a... all the other men in that

95

street were... they all... except this man, who knew...

DAVIE: But how did he know?

VI: Something about his routine.

DAVIE: But they all do that. Like I said. You need your concentration.

VI: Do what?

DAVIE: Have a routine.

VI: Yes. Yes, of course. They all do it. Of course. How's the fire?

DAVIE: I'll check.

[Davie goes to check the fire. Vi looks out to sea, the memory still stirring.]

Goin' down fast. There'll be nothing left.

VI: Where's England from here?

DAVIE: Straight across. Round the southern edge of Newfoundland and keep going.

VI: Go home now, Davie. Take the car. *[she takes money from her wallet]* Get your sister to a doctor.

DAVIE: I can't.

VI: Just take it.

DAVIE: Let me wait and drive you back.

VI: The walk'll do me good.

DAVIE: It may not be safe for you, though. There may be trouble tonight.

VI: There's nothing they can do to hurt me. Go on, now.

[Davie takes the money.]

DAVIE: I'll pay you back. *[he goes to leave, then hesitates]* The boys who threw the flour... I found out who they were. I knew one of them back then, but I couldn't... one of them was my brother.

VI: I see.

DAVIE: The others have left now. All gone. So you don't have to worry. This used to be a place to come to. Now it's a place to leave. I couldn't tell you at the time. I'm sorry. But I made sure it didn't happen again.

           [Davie leaves. Vi steps to the edge of the cliff and looks down. She spreads her arms like wings. Will appears on the cliff behind Vi. He grabs her.]

WILL: Need a push? *[pause]* Getting fat there. *[pause]* Not many round here can say the same.

VI: I can't help that.

WILL: They hate you, don't they?

VI: Do I care?

WILL: Yes.

VI: No. No. I don't. *[pause]* Look at it out here. Just look at it. All this way and it looks like Wales. Just like bloody Wales. *[She laughs then stops.]* Can you tell me my name? Can you? You wouldn't even if you could, would you?

WILL: Your name is William Couth.

VI: My real name. From when I was born.

WILL: Never look back.

VI: No. That's right. *[pause]* It's just that lately I can almost remember... I can almost... No. It's gone again.

WILL: Only look ahead.

VI: Yes. Plan for the future.

97

WILL: What is the plan then?

VI: I don't seem to have one. Things'll take care of themselves here now.

WILL: You mean the army will come in.

VI: I suppose. First sign of trouble.

WILL: At the power plant tonight, perhaps. At the rally.

VI: Maybe.

WILL: Your idea?

VI: Can't remember.

WILL: I think you can.

VI: Maybe. Maybe yes. My idea. They deserve it.

WILL: Who does?

VI: You don't know what they're like. What they did.

WILL: No?

VI: They killed a man. Someone trying to help them. They never respected him.

WILL: I thought the black dust in his lungs killed him.

VI: No. They did. With their pointing at him, and their pity. She's alright, you know. The boy's sister. I gave them money for a doctor.

WILL: Why do that?

VI: She's been ill.

WILL: I thought that was what you wanted.

VI: No.

WILL: Surely that was the whole point.

VI: I didn't know she'd get ill though. That particular girl.

WILL: Well who then?

VI: I don't know. One of them.

WILL: Who?

VI: One of *them!* One of *them!* Can't you — *[she stops abruptly, thinks hard, holds her breath, then loses it, lets it go]* — No. It's gone. I nearly had it there again.

WILL: I hope that little girl doesn't go to the rally tonight.

VI: She won't. She's been ill.

WILL: I hope her father doesn't carry her down there up on his shoulders.

VI: They wouldn't hurt her. She's not one of them.

WILL: It would make her an easy target though, wouldn't it?

VI: They wouldn't hurt her.

WILL: But they might shoot her brother. Or her father from under her.

VI: No, they wouldn't do that. They just wouldn't do it.

WILL: But the soldiers will be there.

VI: They might be.

WILL: You ordered them to be.

VI: I can't help that. I can't change the past.

WILL: Can't you?

VI: No. Go away. What d'you want?

WILL: What do *you* want?

VI: I don't know. When you're not here, where d'you go?

WILL: Nowhere. I'm just not here.

VI: What's it like?

WILL: Peaceful.

VI: That's what I want.

WILL: But then you'd be dead.

           [*Vi thinks.*]

VI: Did I kill you?

WILL: What do you think?

VI: I don't know. I wish you'd go away.

WILL: Why?

VI: Because you make me lonely. I can't have a friend. Even one I made up.

WILL: Why not?

VI: Because I'm special.

           [*With a flourish, Will takes out a pen and a piece of paper. He writes on it. Vi watches. He shows her what he has written.*]

WILL: Know what that says?

VI: No.

WILL: It's your name. Your real name. From when you were born.

VI: Let me see.

           [*He shows her again, but won't let her touch it.*]

WILL: And when I've gone then no one will know it.

VI: What does it say?

WILL: That's what you wanted, isn't it?

VI: Yes, but tell me what it says.

WILL: Nobody here will ever know who you are.

VI: Give it to me now.

WILL: That is what you wanted?

           [*Vi keeps trying to get the paper off him.*]

VI: Yes. I've said, but give it to me.

WILL: Why?

VI: Just give it to me.

WILL: It'll be as if she never existed.

[She starts to fight in earnest for the paper.]

And no one will miss her.

VI: Give me the paper.

[He pushes her away, hard. She falls. He lights the paper from the dying fire. Vi goes berserk. She flies at him and fights him, hard.]

Don't do that! Give it to me! Give it to me!

[She wrestles him to the floor and snatches the paper and slaps out the flames.]

Oh no oh no oh no. There there. There there. Don't hurt her. My name. Oh my name. My name.

[She gets her breath. Will is gone.]

I don't know if I meant to kill you. But I know now I would do it again. I know something happened. There was a man and a woman. And one of them died. But for a long time I couldn't say which. But you were wrong about something. Someone does miss her. I miss her. And another one does also. But I cannot say their names. I've lost my voice, you see.

[Vi folds the charred paper.]

I'll keep her safe here.

[She tucks the paper inside her shirt. Then she remembers something.]

I should warn them. The little girl. I should tell them. I should ring the alarm. I should ring the bells.

[She sets off back to town and breaks into a run. As she exits the bells start to ring.]

SCENE EIGHT

[Vi's room. Vi and Davie. Vi is resigned, Davie, angry.]

DAVIE: But why, sir?

VI: I'm sorry, I just don't need you any more.

DAVIE: I was learning all the time.

VI: No, it's nothing you've done wrong, you're just not needed.

DAVIE: And I always kept your secrets.

VI: I know you can be trusted.

DAVIE: My own family I didn't tell things to because I thought you might be angry.

VI: I can't really help that.

DAVIE: They would ask about you and I'd say nothing. Even when that was hard.

VI: As I say, I won't be needing you again.

DAVIE: And now, with all that's happened...

VI: I've put some money on one side.

DAVIE: I've nothing to go back to.

VI: I think you'll find it generous enough.

DAVIE: I had to make a choice...

VI: It's more than you'd have earned if you'd been here.

DAVIE: And I chose you. I chose to follow you. Believe the things you said.

VI: Well that was very stupid of you.

DAVIE:	Sir?
VI:	Don't call me sir. I'm not your sir. Here's the money. Take it and get out. Go on, get out.
DAVIE:	You knew. You knew about the army.
VI:	Yes.
DAVIE:	And the water?
VI:	I knew about everything. Don't you see?
DAVIE:	So if we hadn't been warned the other night, anything could have happened, and all the time you knew.
VI:	The soldiers are here to stay now, Davie. Keep out of their way. And tell your brothers to do the same. They'll round up any troublemakers.
DAVIE:	Well thanks for the advice.
VI:	You don't know the circumstances....
DAVIE:	I don't know anything any more, Mr Couth. I don't know anything at all.

[Davie leaves.]

SCENE NINE

[The Couth's drawing room. Therese holds the sock ball in her hand. She squeezes it as Su counts.]

SU: (...and six, and seven, and eight. Good. Other hand.)

[Therese changes hands.]

(One and two, and three, and four, and five, and six, and seven, and eight. Good.)

[Therese throws the sock ball to Su, who catches it.]

Oh very clever you are, I must say. Shall I read a bit more then?

[Therese nods. She makes an affirmative sound, not quite a word. Su goes back to the paper she has been reading from earlier. She reads from an ad. The paper is The Times, dated April 21st, 1925. Su's reading is more enthusiastic than fluent.]

"Your legs have met the ordinary kind of gate-leg table — met it painfully. Here, an out of the way gate-leg table just as handy as the ordinary kind, but when it's open, its legs are 'out-of-the-way'. All the difference. Its uses every housewife knows — for tea, for cards, for flowers, indeed all occasional uses. And when it's out of use, you can tuck it in a corner and it still looks nice. Try it for seven days free. Five pound and five bob" — blimey it's not cheap — "or thirty-five bob down and six monthly payments". No ta.

[She turns the page.]

Here's a good one. "Small boys have a horror of being coddled. They like to be independent of girlish nonsense, to feel that they are men and can take care of themselves..."

[Therese waves her hand and makes a mangled "non".]

Just a minute. I'm coming to the good bit. "Mother, the health doctor, encourages this youthful pride. Knowing it is good for their characters, she lets them believe they are quite capable of doing without her..."

[Therese complains again.]

It's for Lifebuoy...?

THERESE: Non.

SU: That's the only one we've not read.

[Therese reaches out for the paper. Su takes it to her. Therese points to the news copy.]

I can't read the proper parts. I'm not good enough.

[Therese begs her.]

Oh alright. What d'you fancy then? Sport?

THERESE: Non.

SU: Weather.

THERESE: Non.

SU: Ballet.

THERESE: Ah!

SU: You want the bit about the ballet?

THERESE: Ah.

SU: Okay. New ballet for... Millie... Kar-sa-vina.

THERESE: Non!

SU: But you asked for it.

[Therese beckons Su to show her the paper. She scans the article. There is something familiar. The abbreviation 'Mlle' which Su has misread as 'Millie'. Slowly Therese tries to form a word.]

THERESE: Mm... mm....

SU: Millie.

THERESE: Ma... Ma... mademoiselle. Mademoiselle.

SU: Yes. Mamsel. Yes, of course. It's short for mamsel. Oh, that's brilliant. You're brilliant, you are. "New ballet for Mamsel Karsavina".

THERESE: Mademoiselle.

SU: Mam-wu-zel.

THERESE: Oui. Oui.

[Therese claps her hands. From this point on, when Therese speaks there is nothing idiotic about her, only the sense that she has not spoken for a long time and it is hard work. She is gradually rediscovering a language.]

She knows no words in the language other than the ones she uses when the right context arises.]

SU: Mam-wu-zel Tamara Karsavina will be seen in a new ballet at the Coliseum next Monday. It is called 'The Happy Deception', and the music is taken from Handel's Water Music, first performed in 1714 at a Royal... Royal... *[she shows the page to Therese]*

THERESE: F... Fete!

SU: Royal fett on the Thames in honour of King George the First's ...ak...ak... *[she shows the page to Therese]*

THERESE: "Accession".

SU: Ak-sess-yon. George the First's ak-sess-yon to the throne. The action is during the period of... *[shows Therese]*

THERESE: Louis Seize

SU: Louis Says.

[She looks at the page and shows it to Therese immediately.]

THERESE: Monsieur... Pierre... Vladimiroff.

SU: ...assists Mam-wu-zell Karsavina in the perform-ance of this ballet.

THERESE: Ballet.

SU: Ballet.

THERESE: Oui.

SU: Ballet, ballet, ballet.

[She kisses Therese.]

Ballet, ballet, ballet.

[Su does balletic hops about the room. Therese claps.]

THERESE: Encore.

SU: I could show that Nijinsky a thing or two, eh?

THERESE: Oui.

[Therese reaches out for her. Su stops dancing.]

SU: What?

[Therese struggles to form a sentence.]

THERESE: Je... je... ne... suis... pas... ...solitaire. Je ne suis pas solitaire.

SU: Sorry?

[Su goes to listen. Therese struggles to explain.]

THERESE: Je... je... *[She points to herself. Su mirrors the action.]*

SU: I?

THERESE: Oui.

SU: I.

THERESE: Je ne suis pas... *[Therese shakes her head, gestures with her hands]*

SU: I won't.

THERESE: Non.

SU: I can't?

THERESE: Non. Je ne suis pas. *[she repeats the gestures]*

SU: I'm not?

THERESE: Oui. Oui. Je ne suis pas solitaire.

SU: I am not... solitaire. Solitaire? Like the ring? Like a ring with one stone?

THERESE: Oui...

SU: I am not... I am not a diamond? *[Therese gives up]* I am not a diamond. Oh, but you are, you know. You are.

[Su holds Therese's hand. There is a moment of real affection between the two.]

SCENE TEN

[Vi's room. She sits in a long shirt, clearly very pregnant. She eats from a tray, using her hands, slides the tray out under the door when she has finished. She picks her teeth. There is a knock on the door which she ignores. There is another knock.]

DAVIE: It's me. Open the door. *[pause]* I'm serious. Open the door. Open the door before I kick it down.

[The door flies open. Davie carries a large bag. He looks at her.]

DAVIE: You're further along than I thought. *[pause]* Here. *[he opens the bag and throws her a dress]* Someone's been shot. The plant was stormed, and the soldiers fired. They'll come looking for you. They think you're involved.

VI: I am.

DAVIE: They'll hurt you. Put that on now.

[Davie gathers up anything useful and throws it into the bag. Vi pulls the dress over her. It is too small.]

I can't believe it took me so long. I mean, look at you.

[He throws her a sweater. She pulls it on slowly.]

There's food in the bag. Not much, but enough. I'll give you a letter. I've a friend has a row-boat down the coast from the cliffs. You can sleep there if you need to. You'll be cold but you'll survive. It's more than you deserve. *[he gives her a letter]* Show it to them at the pier.

VI: What does it say?

DAVIE: Don't mess me about.

VI: Why are you helping me?

DAVIE: Because of my sister. I know what you are.

[Vi takes out the folded paper.]

VI: This is what I am. Read it. *[she unfolds it]*

DAVIE: Violet Evans.

[Vi's belly kicks.]

VI: Violet Evans. *[she remembers]* Susie Owen. *[she laughs and takes back the paper]* Yes. That's what I am.

DAVIE: There isn't time for this.

[Davie continues packing. He tries to force a coat onto an uncooperative Vi.]

VI: There was a man once, and he built boats, and people thought him mad, but that's not how things start. They start with a miner.

DAVIE: You told me.

VI: But on the day of the explosion, he lights his cigarette and the match goes out. He sits in his chair and it strikes cold. So he doesn't die.

DAVIE: Pitsense. I told you they all do it. A match goes out, you're not concentrating. A chair strikes cold you're sickening for something. You have to know yourself or you're a danger. The routine goes wrong you don't go down. There's no magic to it. Just common sense. He prob'ly had a chill.

VI: But he knew.

DAVIE: Maybe afterwards he thought he knew. Survivors get guilty.

VI: But why would men hate him for that?

DAVIE: They wouldn't.

VI: Not him, perhaps, but his family.

DAVIE: I don't know.

VI: The children of the men who died. They hated his child. She was only a child, and they hated her.

DAVIE: That's just kids.

VI: That's it. *[her belly kicks, hard]* That's it. I am not special. I am not special.

DAVIE: You have to get away from here.

VI: I am not special.

[He puts the bag in her hand and pushes her out the door.]

SCENE ELEVEN

[The Couth's drawing room. Therese sits in a proper chair with her eyes closed. It is a sunny June evening. Su's voice calls:]

SU: (No peekin' now.)

THERESE: Non.

SU: (I mean it.)

[Su enters pushing the embroidery frame with a new piece of linen stretched across it. She sets it up where it was before and moves a chair to it. She is wearing a light summer jacket over her dress.]

SU: (Okay — ready, steady, open your eyes.) *[Therese looks at the frame and smiles]* Now. *[Su gives Therese a postcard from her pocket]* This is a view of the beach at Harlech my mam sent me. I thought we'd copy the picture and make something really big and hang it on the wall. We've enough pillow-slips and such t'last a lifetime. What d'you think?

THERESE: Oui.

[Su sorts through her bag which contains many little paper bags.]

SU: Fresh needles, look. And a special pencil for tracing the lines. And... here's the thread. (I brought you all the colours of the sea.)

[She shows Therese the colours. Therese fingers them with pleasure. Su puts all the bags with the frame and waits for Therese. Therese moves herself to the edge of the chair and tries to stand, leaning on her cane. Su gives her a gentle hand then backs away. Therese moves slowly to the other chair, with Su ready to catch her should she stumble. Seated, Therese runs her hands over the taut fabric. She calls Su to sit next to her.]

THERESE: Viens ici.

[Su moves a chair and sits beside her.]

SU: Now I can't draw for toffee, so you'll have to start.

[Therese starts to draw, carefully and with difficulty. Su refers to the postcard and advises. Above Su and Therese, Vi squats in a little boat. The bell rings erratically in the distance. She is in labour and in pain, but controlled, determined. Her groans build to a crescendo, until she cries out in triumph and the baby is born.]

[Therese has drawn a rough outline. She fills in the detail.]

SU: It'll be something to remind me of home, you see. We can do one of France after, if you like.

THERESE: Oui. *[knowing the misunderstanding involved]* Je ne suis pas solitaire.

SU: Nonsense madame. You're a little gem.

[Therese laughs and returns to her work.]

[Vi holds a bundle in her arms and cradles it. Her accent has returned.]

VI: My name is Violet Evans. I am complete. I am intact. I am all present. Nothing but present. But what shall you be called? What name shall you be given?

        [Therese has finished her drawing. She dozes in her chair. Su takes a pencil from her hands and looks at the postcard.]

VI: Shall I call you Newfoundland for our first port of call? Or shall you be named for the first fish we see? I had a name I would have called you if you'd been born a girl. Look at the water, how it's a mirror. There are stars in the sea, there are fish in the sky. Can you read what they say? They say south, they say east, they say home.

        [Su sits on the floor sorting the different embroidery threads into colours. She sings softly to herself, a Welsh lullaby. Vi strokes her baby's hair.]

SU: I tell you, Mrs Couth, at the end of the day, you and I will not be judged by whether or not our people come home. We will be judged by the quality of our waiting. *[she lays the coloured threads in a semi-circle]*

VI: Sometimes you look out at the sea and it's...

SU: Blue.

VI: Sometimes you look out at the sea and it's...

SU: Grey.

VI: Sometimes you look out at the sea and it's...

SU: Black. White.

VI: Some days you look out and it's...

SU: Green, like a starling.

VI: But one day, you look out at the sea, and it's...

SU: Waiting.

[Su takes the magnet from her pocket and places it on the floor in the semi-circle of wool.]

Magnets and prayers. Who's to say the one can't be the other. Poor Vi. Always looking for meanings. But she'll come home alright. You see the meaning was right under her nose all the time. It was me. It was me.

[Su smiles, full of love. Closes her eyes and feels the end of the day's sun on her face. Vi casts off. She takes up the little oars.]

VI: (Hush now, angel. Don't be afraid.) For there's nothing to be frightened of. (Shshshsh. Shshshsh.)

[The sound of the little oars in the water, as the lights fade.]

The End

The Author

Lucinda Coxon was born in Derby in 1962. She has written plays for and worked with writers' groups at a number of theatres including Loose Exchange Theatre Co., the Royal Court, Tricycle, Cockpit and Bush Theatres. *Waiting at the Water's Edge* has been performed at the Bush Theatre as well as the Ohio Theatre Space in New York. Made in Wales will be producing the play in Wales in 1995. Her stage adaptation of Tarjei Vessaas novel, *The Ice Palace*, was commissioned by the Royal National Theatre in 1994. Lucinda has also written a single drama for the BBC — *Eddie's Proposal*, and two feature screenplays: *Spaghetti Show* and *Lily and the Secret Planting*. She has delivered a new play for the Bush theatre, *Wishbones*, and is currently writer in residence at the Mercury Theatre, Colchester and the University of Essex.

Note To The Series

Welsh drama found a new and distinctive voice in the eighties. Before that, there were new theatres in Wales, but there was little new drama. Why was it that there was a surge of new writing at this time? Perhaps it is no accident that the decade was one of economic hardship and unemployment. It would not be the first time that adversity has brought the best out of the Welsh. We can be certain, however, that new writers were sustained by the commitment of a band of theatre professionals, many of whom shared with them a common background and experience. During this period, new writers have been specifically fostered by the Made in Wales Stage Company. This academy of stage writing has had a crucial training role, enabling emerging dramatists to learn through workshops and the experience of seeing their plays performed in front of an audience. Other companies, such as Hijinx, The Sherman Theatre, Theatre Clwyd, Moving Being, Y Cwmni, and others, have commissioned new plays and/or taken them to community venues to people who would normally find theatres alien and intimidating. Welsh dramatists have benefited directly from this professional support system and indirectly from the patronage of public bodies but they have not yet reached the audiences that they deserve. Irish theatre-goers have in the past greeted new writers with riots, and today they still provide the oxygen of controversy, but if the attendance at some Welsh premieres is any indication, innovation in Wales meets with indifference from the public at large.

Seren, with the support of the Arts Council of Wales, are pleased to publish a series of new plays which will facilitate re-staging, enhance the status of new dramatists, and, we hope, help draw new audiences into our theatres. We cannot afford, nor would it be proper, to limit support to a movement or faction, if any exists. To the list of writers who were born in Wales, or who now live here, we will add the name of any writer of quality, who makes his or her initial breakthrough before Welsh audiences.

There are a number of questions that need to be answered about the present state of our theatre. Just how good are our writers? Is the neglect of English managements evidence of discrimination, or merely of lack of knowledge? Are we at last beginning to create a national theatre that will one day equal those of Scotland and Ireland? We hope that the publication of this drama series will help to find the answers.

Brian Mitchell
Editor